Rock of Ages

Memories of the Past,

A Legacy for the Future

WRITE TOGETHER™ PUBLISHING
Nashville, Tennessee

Copyright © 2000
by the Tennessee Association of Homes and Services for the Aging (TNAHSA).

All rights reserved.

Published by Write Together™ Publishing LLC.
www.writetogether.com

ISBN 1-930142-58-7

Title: Rock of Ages: Memories of the Past, A Legacy for the Future. Subject: 20th Century literary collections; Tennessee senior authors. (Multiple authors).

Project sponsor:	Tennessee Association of Homes and Services for the Aging (TNAHSA).
500 Interstate Blvd., South
Nashville, TN 37201
615-256-1800

Project coordinators:	Doug Pace, President, TNAHSA
Yeolanda Dowlen, Executive Assistant

Publisher:	Paul Clere, Write Together Publishing

Editor:	John D. Bauman

Cover and Book Design:	Bill Perkins

To publish a book for your not-for-profit organization that complements your values, vision and mission, please contact

Write Together™ Publishing
533 Inwood Dr.
Nashville, TN 37211

phone: 615-781-1518
fax: 520-223-4850

www.writetogether.com

TABLE OF CONTENTS

Foreword 1

Chapter 1 Our Memories

Jean Waldron **Winter Memories in Tennessee** 4
Grace Dixon **The Year of the Interurban** 4
Helen Cureton **Christmas Eve**..5
James Cornelius Hundley **Putting Mail on Trains** 7
Lucy Mizell **A Summer Memory** 7
Roy Henry **1941 Before Inflation** 8
Mary Becherer **A Turbulent Period in Detroit History**..9
Ernest B. Trotter **A Trip on the *Queen Elizabeth I***...10
Paul Nolan **Payment in Kind** 11
Reba A. Fitzgerald **Memories of Teaching**...12
Geneva F. Bouchard **Those Were the Days**..12
Jeanette Levey **Lakota** 14
Helen Potts **A River Outing**..15
Dorothy Morris **A Story** 16
Irene Berry **Memories of Life on the Farm... and Beyond** 16
Lalise M. O'Brien **Mountains and Fried Chicken**..17
Bruce Monroe **The Roaring Twenties**...19
Joanne Smalling **My Aunt Bessie** 20
Helen Baker Muccio **A "Greenhorn" Celebrates Ninety Years in the USA**......22
James Cornelius Hundley **My First Day of School**..25
Irene Berry **My Long Lost First Love** 25
Faith Cornwall **The Bear and I**..26
Mardelle S. Bourdon **Old Do-It-Yourselfers Never Die, They Just Roll Off the Roof**...27
Lester A. Ludlow **The Sweet Pits**..28
Sara S. Shipley **Devoted Listening** 29
Marietta Dickerson **Extending the Dinner Table**..29
Ruth R. Broyles **Terry's New Challenge** 30
Bruce Monroe **A Humbling Experience** 31
Gladys Gilliam Fillers **A Travel in Time**..31
Clara Anniss McCartt **Reflecting on Reaching Age Ninety** 33

Chapter 2 Our Selves

Biography of Christine Lamb McMahon 36
Biography of James Ozment 36
Biography of Willie Mae Brown 37
Biography of Persis Grayson..37

Biography of Catherine Ries 38
Biography of Mary Lou McDonough 39
Biography of Pearl Huntley 39
Biography of Ruth Hurt 40
Biography of Nancy Britton 41

Chapter 3 Our Lives

Alma Rule **Assisted Living** 44
Alma Rule **Victorian Square** 44
Dorothy Brown **Oh, What a Nice Place This Is** 45
Harold Russell **Assisted Living** 46
Juanita Vaughan **The Joy of Retirement** 47

Chapter 4 Our Lessons

Mary West **How Old Are You?** 50
Austin Flint Hubbard **I Led Three Lives** 51
James Wendell Wooten **Healthcare from Heaven** 53
Ena Eble Peavyhouse **"Let's Have a Party"** 53
Lucille Skaggs **All About Jesus** 54
M.C. Morriss Keller **Synonyms** 55
Florence Irwin **In Quietness** 56

Chapter 5 Our Words

Ruby McDill **Twilight** 60
Sherry S. Haney **Siblings** 60
Rose Love Tate **Ode to a Tree** 61
Rubye Longley Hundley **Hands** 61
Mardelle S. Bourdon **In the Mining Museum** 62
Lily Hardy **To Wait for a Train** 63
Charlotte H. Alexander **Yellow Butterfly** 63
Lily Hardy **He Was Taking Her Home at Twilight** 63
Sherry S. Haney **Saturday Morning** 64
Jeanette Mandigo **Noon-Time** 64
Rose Love Tate **Reasons for Love** 64
Sterling Brownlow **We, the People** 65
Mardelle S. Bourdon **Where are the Fairies?** 65
Juanita Vaughan **The Days Between** 66
Sherry S. Haney **Numbers** 67
Frank Willson **Yellow Rose** 68
Rubye Longley Hundley **Grandmother to Granddaughter** 68
Sterling Brownlow **The Statue of Liberty** 69
Vera Maye Ward **One Magic Hour** 70
Juanita Vaughan **Love, Joe** 70
Mary Shires **Words** 71
Rose Love Tate **Bondage** 71
Doris Davis **If I Were Skilled** 71
Juanita Vaughan **The Prodigal Son** 72

Rose Love Tate **The Future**..73
Mardelle S. Bourdon **Summer's End**..73

Chapter 6 Our Faith

Mary L. Chapman **He is Here!**...76
Charlotte Zotti **A Rose is Like a Beautiful Face**...................................77
Mildred R. Strahley **O, World I Love You So!**......................................77
Joyce Huey Salyer **God's Love**..78
Sterling Brownlow **A Thanksgiving Prayer**...79
Clara Wright **I Wonder**..80
Phyllis E. Haire **An Ecclesiasticus of Our Day**....................................80
Hildred Hardin **Trees**..81
Janella Kirk **Prayer of a Vain Student**...83
Juanita Vaughan **Scarlet Ribbon of Pain**..83
Sterling Brownlow **Easter**..84
Amber Simmons **My Little Angel**..85
Juanita Vaughan **Captain of my Fate**...85
Sherry S. Haney **Progress?**..86
Edna Buchanan **Struggle**...86
Joyce Huey Salyer **Flawless**...87
Colbert Petrie **Now - I Live**...88
Faith Cornwall **Ascent**..89
Amber Simmons **Mother**...89
Rose Love Tate **Now I Lay Me Down to Sleep**....................................90
Ann Anderson **The Hand of God**...91

Chapter 7 Our Past

Pearl Huntley **Memory Lane**..94
Sterling Brownlow **Re-cycled**...94
Pearl Huntley **Yon End and Back**...95
Merle Stanton **Thanksgiving Stomach Ache**.......................................95
Mary Miller **Learning to Drive**...96
Pearl Huntley **Courting in Cardboard Soles**.......................................97
Rose Love Tate **A Christmas Gift**...98

FOREWORD

We hope you enjoy this collection of stories, letters and poetry from residents of TNAHSA (Tennessee Association of Homes and Services for the Aging) member facilities. This anthology of poetry and prose contains a small but powerful representation of the imagination, vitality, creativeness, and talent of our elderly generation. Our Tennessee seniors share their diverse thoughts and insights on a variety of themes ranging from memories of youth, the importance of faith, aging in today's society, life in assisted living facilities, and more. This collection serves as a reminder that the issues of relevance and importance to our senior population are in reality issues that impact all Tennesseans.

TNAHSA represents over 200 skilled nursing facilities, nursing facilities, assisted care living facilities, homes for the aged, independent and HUD housing, continuing care retirement communities, and home and community based service providers across the state of Tennessee.

The mission of TNAHSA is to represent and promote the common interests of its members through leadership, advocacy, education, communication and other services in order to enhance members' ability to serve their constituencies.

As community leaders, partners, and stakeholders, TNAHSA members work with other associations, civic and community groups, professional organizations and legislators to develop a model of a high quality, comprehensive, affordable, accessible and seamless system of caring for older and chronically ill persons emphasizing individual personal choice in selecting services.

Older adults are one of our most precious resources. Let us continue to learn from them, honor them, and work to ensure a healthy, happy quality of life for all.

Richard Lewis
Chair
Tennessee Association of Homes and Services for the Aging

CHAPTER I

OUR MEMORIES

Listen to the older adults of Tennessee as they share their lives and experiences from the last century. Their memories span the age of the greatest change in the history of mankind, and their knowledge of how life used to be and the ways it has changed is an invaluable resource that must not be forgotten.

ROCK OF AGES

Winter Memories In Tennessee
Jean Waldron
Christian Towers and The Manor of Gallatin
Gallatin

Back many years ago it seemed that the winters were much colder than today. It may have been because we did not have the conveniences of today.

Before dark there were things to be done to prepare for the next morning. Since we burned coal in our fireplace and cooked on a coal-fired stove, the coal buckets had to be filled with coal. People who lived on farms usually used wood instead of coal.

Before we went to bed we would lay a flat iron in front of the fireplace to get it hot. Mother would then wrap it in a heavy towel and put in our bed at our feet to help us stay warm while we went to sleep. We slept upstairs where it was very cold. We slept on a feather mattress that helped keep us warm during cold winters. How cold would it get? The water bucket in the kitchen would always be frozen when we got up in the mornings.

We did not have indoor plumbing. So, whether rain, sleet, or snow, there was always a fast run to the outhouse out back. It was also before the days of Charmin, but we did have the Sears and Roebuck catalogue.

When the cold wind would blow, it would come in through a big crack under the door. We would try to stop it by putting some old rags or other items in the crack to stop the cold air from hitting our feet. This was, of course, before the days of Ace Hardware and Home Depot.

When it snowed and Drakes Creek (now known as Old Hickory Lake) would freeze over, we played on the ice. It was deep water, and if the ice had broken it would have been terrible. But, we only thought of the fun we were having playing on the ice.

The coldest winters I can remember were January 1940 and the blizzard of 1951. In 1940 the Cumberland River froze over. People actually walked across the ice from Hendersonville to Old Hickory.

Tennessee is a wonderful place to live. And, if you don't like the weather, just hang around, it will soon change.

The Year of the Interurban
Grace Dixon
Christian Towers and The Manor of Gallatin
Gallatin

It all began in a little one-room school in Allen County, Kentucky.

Although I was only four years old at the time, the teacher agreed to let me attend. My teacher thought that I knew how to read, but I learned the books by heart. I had listened very closely to the other children recite their lessons. I had learned by listening.

The next year my family began to move about. We moved first to Illinois, then to Texas, and finally, when I was six, to Tennessee. I was not able to attend school during these moves, so my mother continued to teach me at home.

When we moved to Sumner County, Tennessee, there was no school near where we lived. My parents got permission for me to attend a school in Hendersonville. There were no school buses in those days; however, the Nashville-Gallatin Interurban, an electric trolley, passed in front of our house. My mother arranged for me to ride it to school every day, and the conductor agreed to see that I got off at the Hendersonville School stop. Mother bought a monthly ticket book, and being afraid that I would lose the ticket book before the month was over, she fastened it to a ribbon and made me wear it around my neck. I had never ridden the Interurban alone before, and I will never forget how the conductor and engineer took such good care of me.

The school was a big, brick building. My first teacher's name was Miss Nannie. She was a tiny lady who wore high-heeled shoes. I loved her from the first day. At first I was started back in primer, but I quickly went through that and then first and second grade, all in the same year.

One day in late winter I came to the school and noticed that there were no children in the school yard as there usually were. I got to the door and it was locked. "Oh, no," I thought. "What am I going to do?" Fortunately my uncle had heard that the school was closed because the steam furnace was being repaired, and he came and got me. I went to his house until it was time to catch the Interurban back home that afternoon.

By the next fall when school was ready to start, we had moved to a small house just a few yards from the school. It was a new experience to be able to just walk to school. But, I will never forget the year of the Interurban!

Christmas Eve

Helen Cureton
Alexian Village of Tennessee
Signal Mountain

A call came from downstairs: "It is time to get up." My father's call meant the four of us must be up, dressed, faces and hands washed and hair combed by the time he finished necessary dairy chores.

Home for the weekend was usually a welcome respite from school in the city, but this particular holiday was another first in our family. It was our first Christmas Eve without Mama.

The housekeeper had gone to her home for the holidays. Her departure left the preparation of meals to me. Just turned fifteen and the oldest of four girls, I was responsible for keeping this special season as normal as possible.

The damp, foggy morning was brightened with chatter from the two youngest children who were eager to finish their breakfasts and get started to the woodland to find a Christmas tree.

The gray fog began to lift as the five of us set out to find a tree that met the approval of four girls. After the short leafed pine was selected and cut, Papa found a wild holly and spruce pine from which he carefully pruned branches for living room decorations.

Home again to a house without a greeting from Mama. The absence of a plate of sugar cookies, steaming mugs of hot chocolate and a whirr from the egg beater signifying preparations for fresh coconut cake cast a spell of silence and sadness.

ROCK OF AGES

Our spirits lifted when Papa brought the tree into the house and boxes of ornaments were unpacked. Familiar possessions, lovingly wrapped after Epiphany was celebrated the previous year, brought cries of joy as each bauble was placed on the floor. Yards of gold and silver tinsel, paper chains, cornucopias, stars covered with tinfoil and a tree top ornament were divided between the four of us.

After the last glass ball was hung, our baby sister, age four, was hoisted high enough to place the large silver and tinsel star on the treetop. It was Papa's turn to share in the fun. He brought from the attic a box of tin candleholders and candles. These were secured in strategic spots for a brief lighting when evening came.

The bright flames from the fireplace made our efforts so beautiful no one wanted to leave the room. We had lunch in a semicircle allowing ourselves pride in a masterpiece our minds and hands created.

The evening came swiftly with clear crisp beauty. We prepared for a short walk to the Community Church for a special Christmas Eve service. Perhaps our brother would join us there after a business meeting in the city.

Too soon the service ended. Carols were sung; an account of the birth of our Lord according to St. Luke was read; the first grade angel choir sang "Away in the Manger." Finally the ubiquitous Santa Claus delivered tarlatan stockings filled with candy, nuts and one orange.

The walk home began. The moon was full and the stars seemed bigger and brighter than ever before. My mind kept racing back to the Star of Bethlehem and God's gift of the Holy Child. I couldn't think of one gift I had ever given Him.

After hanging our stockings we were anxious to get to bed. Papa gave each a kiss on the cheek but hesitated when it was my turn. He said, "Sister wait, I want to talk to you." He left the room to return with his arms filled with dolls, games, assorted packages and five books the same size and color. Another trip to a back room brought forth a box of fruit, nuts and stocking fillers. He began to sob, "I am so sorry, you will have to fill the stockings and arrange the gifts. I can't do it without your mother."

I was alone standing in front of the fireplace. I was angry. How could he spoil my Christmas? Now, all the magic of Christmas morning would be gone. What joy is left if I see my gifts before the others? Why doesn't my brother have to do this?

As I shed copious quantities of tears, I filled the stockings with the usual contents I always liked to find on Christmas morning, but this time there will be just three to be surprised.

The joys, dolls, and wrapped packages were arranged. The identical books still in one stack intrigued me. I removed the top volume. The title in bold letters almost jumped at me. In gold was "The Holy Bible." I opened the first flyleaf. On it was written: "To Helen, my eldest daughter. From your father 1921." How good of him to remember that Mama always gave each of us a special book for Christmas.

All of a sudden my tears ceased to flow. My anger subsided and I felt the warmth of my mother's presence. Did she want me to realize I had just given the gift of love to all of her dear ones?

OUR MEMORIES

Putting Mail on Trains
James Cornelius Hundley
McKendree Village
Hermitage

    Since the U.S. Post Office was in our store and dad was the Postmaster, we had to take care of the mail. This meant hanging the mailbags so that the speeding trains could use their hook to catch the mailbag. At least one train per day each way had to have the mail hung for them and one per day each way stopped for mail and passengers. The engineer, perhaps in cahoots with the conductor, got in a bad habit of letting the train only slow down and roll on down the tracks. I wanted to be helpful and ran, almost frantically at first, carrying the sometimes heavy mailbags down the track a good distance. I decided it was a game with them to see how far they could make me run. I finally got enough of this and started just standing in the station yard and motioning the train to back up to me, with the mail car door even with where I was standing. A few times of making them back the train up to me cured them and they started stopping where they were supposed to stop.

A Summer Memory
Lucy Mizell
Morningside of Franklin
Franklin

    We were not a beach family, but we did have a swimming pool in Franklin on Lewisburg Pike. It was called Willow Plunge. What a beautiful, fun place to spend a long summer day.
    Large willows hung over the two pools, one a kiddie pool and the other a regular. Both were fed by a spring. The admission price was $.25, but if you knew the boy at the gate, you might just get in free. It cost $.10 for a locker in the locker rooms and there was of course a girls' side and a boys' side. There were knotholes in the walls, so you might see a pair of boy's eyes peeping in, and I'm sure it happened the other way around also.
    The parking lot was on top of a long sloping hill, which went to the pools. Especially on the weekends, you could hardly find a place for a towel to sun yourself after having a dip in the pool.
    They had a wonderful small concession stand, where they cooked fresh, delicious hamburgers and mouth watering homemade individual chess pies.
    They had a juke box, which played all the "oldies" of the 40's and 50's and could be heard all over the hill. Back behind the jukebox, in the shade, was a miniature golf course. Everyone enjoyed playing that.
    Fun was always had at Willow Plunge, even the sunburn!!!

ROCK OF AGES

1941 Before Inflation
Roy Henry
McKendree Village
Hermitage

When I was a young teenager, growing up in Blue Ridge, Georgia, I spent one summer vacation working for my brother who owned a service station. One day I noticed a newspaper on his desk advertising the Joe Louis vs. Billy Conn Fight being held at the Polo Grounds in New York City. I wanted to see this fight, but I could not afford a trip to New York.

That same day, a gentleman driving a van pulled into the station going to Passaic, New Jersey. He must have heard my conversation with my brother about the fight because he offered me a ride to New Jersey. My brother, who was ten years my senior, encouraged me to take advantage of this opportunity. He gave me $10.00 for my expenses, and I withdrew $10.00 from my meager savings account. With one change of clothing and $20.00, I was in the co-pilot seat of that van.

I enjoyed going to places that I had heard of, but the prime place was the Washington Truck Stop. They served excellent food at a reasonable price, especially the soup, which cost ten cents a bowl. When my van driver friend left me in Passaic, I took a bus to New York City for less than $2.00. There I inquired about the YMCA because of its reputation and economical prices. I was informed that there was no YMCA but that there was a similar institution called the Sloan House, and the cost was fifty cents a night. I stayed one night and had an enjoyable stay.

During my travel I became acquainted with a gentleman who was from New York and who knew the city quite well. I informed him that I had very little knowledge of New York and had meager means to pay a tour guide. He was kind enough to give me a tour for free.

I recall going to Radio City Music Hall and seeing the famous high stepping Rockettes. Jack Dempsey was performing at a bar room, and that same day I saw Mickey Walker, Madison Square Garden, and the Empire State Building.

I saw Joe DiMaggio hit a home run in Yankee Stadium. Well, after the game it was fight time at the Polo Grounds. After the fight ended, I grabbed my bag and caught a bus to Washington, D.C. There I looked for two things: the truck stop where I had eaten before and a truck driver going to Blue Ridge, Georgia. I was fortunate to catch a ride with a truck driver in Washington, D.C., hauling peaches to Ft. Valley, Georgia. From there, I hitchhiked a ride to the Farmer's Market in Atlanta. By this time, I was anxious to get back home after being away for almost a week. I also wanted to brag about my experience in New York.

I returned back home to Blue Ridge, Georgia, via Smokey Mountain Trailways and I still had $8.00 left, which I deposited back into my savings account.

OUR MEMORIES

A Turbulent Period in Detroit History
Mary Becherer
Alexian Village of Tennessee
Signal Mountain

After dating for four years through the depression, Ray and I were married in 1937. Jobs were scarce and, for future security job-wise and a better salary, Ray applied to the Civil Service for a position with either the Detroit Police or Fire Department. He passed all the examinations and was put on the waiting list. At that time, he was earning about $50.00 per week. I was also working as a secretary, a nine-hour day, earning $22.50 per week. He finally was called by the Fire Department to start a six-week training period with ten in his class.

His class included the first two black trainees of the Civil Service of the Detroit Police and Fire Department. This, of course, caused a rumble throughout the city from the Mayor and City Council, the Fire Commission down to all the department heads. There was picketing at the training school, protests, radio commentaries and a great deal of animosity and finger pointing as to who was responsible for allowing this to happen. These two recruits were hand-picked, very intelligent, physically in great shape and very articulate. They were able to handle all the requirements and pass all exams.

The ten trainees had a rigid and difficult schedule. They covered handling fire equipment, climbing to the sixth floor of a building on extension ladders, carrying sandbags to test their capacity to rescue occupants. They also had to attend a half-day of classes each day. It was a very intensive program, particularly because of the two black trainees.

The class of ten all graduated and the plan was to integrate them throughout the city at various Engine and Ladder companies so they would be working with experienced fire fighters and learning, as they say, "the ropes." When the Department Chief and Fire Commission assigned these recruits, the Engine and Ladder companies refused to accept a black man into their company. They worked 24-hour shifts and none wanted to sleep in the dorms with them, eat with them or have to socialize with them. The Commission then decided to vacate one engine house and put all the class there, five men on each unit, one of them black, and put a Captain on each shift to head them. The Captain slept in the dorm with the white men and the black man slept in the Captain's quarters.

The first day they went on the job at Engine 34 they found the entire building had been stripped of everything. There was nothing in the kitchen; all dishes, silverware, pots and pans, cleaning equipment, linens, staples and recreational equipment were gone. The previous group of firemen had given everything away to the neighbors surrounding the firehouse. There was picketing, verbal insults, stones thrown and attempted vandalism of their cars. The hatred was shameful! The new recruits had to call their families to bring them a 24-hour supply of food. Gradually, with the help of their families and pooling their money, they were able to refurbish the place so they could cook a meal. All this time the picketing and verbal abuse continued. If they got a call to a fire, people followed with their cars and threw anything they could get their hands on. At one fire because of the lack of experienced firefighters, the house burned down and two occupants lost their lives.

This was a very traumatic and turbulent time in Detroit history, with many small riots and two large ones that burned out entire neighborhoods requiring the

ROCK OF AGES

National Guard to take over. What was once a beautiful city was destroyed by two factions.

Eventually my husband was promoted to the Fire Marshall's office. The two black men, Taylor and White, who were the first to integrate the Civil Service in their class, became Chiefs of their Battalions, had distinguished careers until retirements and were admired and respected by all who worked with them.

A Trip on the *Queen Elizabeth I*
Ernest B. Trotter
The Lodge at Wood Village
Sweetwater

In 1942 I was drafted into the Army and was sent to Jefferson Barracks, Missouri, for Basic Training. After thirteen weeks of training, we were sent to Richmond Army Air Base for Operational Training as the 861st Aviation Engineer Battalion. After the training, which was very extensive, we shipped out to New York, able to do anything in the construction or upkeep of an army air base. They loaded us aboard the *Queen Elizabeth I* to cross the North Atlantic to Europe. She was quite a ship, and we heard there were 22,000 troops aboard when she sailed. She traveled at 30 knots and changed course every mile or so. The reason for the "zig-zag" course was so the German Wolf Packs could not zero their torpedoes on us.

The *Queen Elizabeth* was built to be a luxury liner. Its first use was as a troop-carrying ship. There were twelve men assigned to each stateroom, plus their equipment. There were three triple bunks in each stateroom. Six men would use the bunks for 24 hours, then the other six would take over.

When we did not have a bunk, we would sleep in a hallway or on the deck. It was a hectic trip, but we made it to Greenock, Scotland on the seventh day. Our battalion was given the job of policing the boat. We found all kinds of equipment in the staterooms, personal and military – one 18-wheeler load, I guess. Then we disembarked from the *Queen* and started our journey to England. England was under a very strict blackout. Even the trains were blacked out. We enjoyed the countryside as we traveled and the people gave us kindly welcome. The stations would be full of people to wave at and talk to. We unloaded at Chelmsford and boarded G.I. trucks for the trip to Boreham, which was about ten miles. There were tents put up for us to live in, which held six men to a tent. That night a few German bombers hit Chelmsford and the railroad station. We thought that they had our number and were after us. We had no casualties, but we were scared out of our wits. That night was nothing compared to what we would see in the next year.

OUR MEMORIES

Payment in Kind

Paul Nolan
Alexian Village of Tennessee
Signal Mountain

Following completion of my medical internship at the Tampa, Florida, Municipal Hospital on David Island, Anne and I were married and went to a small mill town in the Western Piedmont section of North Carolina to begin my medical practice in the village of Lawndale. The mill wanted a doctor, so we rented one of the nicer mill homes for the grand sum of $15.00 per month, including water and power. The local druggist needed a physician to write prescriptions to help his business, so an adjoining office was provided, rent-free, and an office nurse was hired at $150.00 per month. I was in business.

Lawndale was a nice little town surrounded by farmland which primarily produced cotton for a cash crop. Many of my patients were sharecroppers, black, and white, landlords, and the usual merchants, mechanics, and other individuals providing various types of services. As luck would have it, that year was a bad year for the boll weevil and the crop was below average. Therefore the money supply was also below average, which was already rather sparse in a normal year.

One of the aspects of my practice which I did not much care for was doing home obstetrics, a long standing procedure since the nearest hospital was about 12 miles away and most patients had no insurance and little cash. I had many interesting experiences delivering babies, who were given interesting names such as Shirley Temple, Joe Louis, Gene Autry, Franklin Roosevelt, George Washington, and, on one occasion, Paul. A great many of these people, if they could pay my $35 fee, could not pay until the "crop was made"–and sold. Sometimes I got paid with "in kind" services or various items. One man paid for the delivery of his child by building a cedar chest for me. Another paid with a very tasty country ham.

One day I went to a home to deliver a child to a family I had never met. This was not unusual, though, for many patients did not contact me until they were in labor. The father-to-be met me at the end of his road, escorted me to his house and apologized profusely that he did not have the money to pay me now, but went to great lengths to tell me how honest he was and always paid his debts. To show me how serious he was about this, he pointed to a cow standing out by his barn and told me that he was going to give me a mortgage on that cow until I was paid. I quickly told him that I did not need the mortgage and I certainly didn't need the cow. I went on into the house, delivered the baby and, on leaving, was presented with the mortgage with the assurance that the money would soon be forthcoming. In spite of my protests, I was now the mortgage holder on a fine milk cow.

When I arrived back at my office and was starting in the door I saw the owner of the furniture store across the street and commented on my good fortune in now almost being in the dairy business. When he asked who the new father was and I told him, he began to laugh so loud he could hardly speak. He said, "You're not going to get in the livestock business – I have the first mortgage on that cow. You only have the second mortgage."

I never saw anything further of that family.

Oh well, I didn't want a cow anyway. Neither Anne nor I knew how to milk.

ROCK OF AGES

Memories of Teaching
Reba A. Fitzgerald
The Courtyard
Dayton

    I am a retired elementary school teacher with a wealth of memories from the classroom. I began teaching before state laws were strict about the number of students in one classroom. I started my teaching career with half the students in a two-teacher school. Nobody told me that it couldn't be done, so I enjoyed doing it that year and the next twenty-one years.

    Many humorous classroom happenings I remember. One was the time when I had twin girls from a family whose church members did not eat certain meats. When we had those meats for lunch, the lady in the kitchen always gave the little girls a slice of cheese instead of meat. One inquisitive little boy asked me why the twins got cheese on their plates, and I told him that the people who go to church where they go didn't eat that kind of meat. So when he got meat that he didn't like he yelled, "Teacher, the people who go to my church don't eat this kind of meat."

    Another memory is from a day just like many school days. One of my early duties was to collect lunch money from the students who waited their turn around my desk. A little boy whom I will call "Honest Abe" was in that group. On that morning I screwed the lid on the money jar that contained my day's collections and report, and the classroom helper took the jar to the cafeteria. The day continued in its usual way. It was years later that "Honest Abe" knocked on my door. I had been retired for many years, and he had grown to become a successful businessman. By that time, his family and mine had a mutual relative whose child had experienced severe medical problems and expenses. During the Christmas holidays he and his siblings' families had decided to use their gift-exchange money as a contribution to the family for medical expenses. He had come by my house to give me the money for that family. Then he took something else from his pocket and said, "This is for you." It was a $100 bill. The story he told me was that when he was in my classroom he saw me counting lunch money and saw a dollar bill fall to the floor. Nobody else had seen it, so he picked it up and put it in his pocket.

    Taking the money had bothered him for many years. Now he wanted to give me this hundred dollars for the dollar he had kept. We still have "Honest Abe's" dollar today!

Those Were The Days
Geneva F. Bouchard
Alexian Village of Tennessee
Signal Mountain

    In the early 1900s, my sister and I lived with our parents in the small village of Loris, South Carolina, near the coast. It was a small farm community, but from it came leaders and statesmen – men of integrity who earned their living by the sweat of their brow, with a firm faith in God.

OUR MEMORIES

My first recollection, at two years, was moving to Charleston, South Carolina, in 1917. During World War I, my Daddy worked for the Railroad and we lived in Charleston. Soon after the war, we moved back near the coast. Eventually, our family increased to five sisters and three brothers. Being next to the eldest, I assumed the role of big brother.

Some of the fondest memories of my early years are of living close to grandparents, cousins, aunts, and uncles. Much of our social life was through our church. Life was simple but we lived happily. All the wealth of happiness we children grew up with would not have been ours without the knowledge that a protecting love surrounded us in our home full of children, our church and our community.

On an acre of ground, we grew our own garden. My parents believed in growing a large garden, and in having a cow and chickens to have a plentiful supply of milk, butter, and eggs. And we were always able to share the bounty with neighbors. Except for going to school camp for a week, my summers were spent helping with canning vegetables from our garden and making jams and jellies. We were taught to do our work before we could play.

Our toys were mostly homemade, using a lot of imagination. We played a lot of baseball, making our ball from tobacco twine. We were as proud as if it had been a Babe Ruth.

My most cherished memories today are those of our barn. The barns of seventy or more years ago were different. Our barn was made of wood with an A-shaped roof, and wide doors. There were no windows. There was one large room downstairs which stored our "farm treasures" – wagon wheels, wagon seats, singletrees, horse collars, hay forks, and odds and ends. The barn had a stall for our cow and a chicken coop. The hayloft was reached by a steep but sturdy ladder. The loft was a favorite place for our cats to have their kittens. Sometimes we were lucky to find some new baby kittens or a nest full of baby chicks. On the roof rafters were barn swallows who built their cup-shaped mud nests, safe from the cats. We sometimes were horrified to see a big black snake slithering its way noiselessly on a nearby barn sill, not far from the swallow's nest.

On Sunday afternoons, when friends came to visit, the hayloft was a perfect stage for "show and tell," as well as a playground. In the hay, we would dig tunnels and caves for hide and seek. If we grew tired of this, there were many barn sills we could climb, tumble from and get our faces full of hay. And we would finally reach the opening door and jump from the roof, trying to see who could jump the farthest.

The hayloft holds special remembrances as a very special playground, replete with magic and make-believe. Nothing is forever, though. The years have gone by, and the time is past for the barns, as I knew them with their many fun and thrilling activities.

In 1920, my Dad bought our first car – a Model T Ford touring car. What a thrill it was to go places in an automobile! In winter, we usually reverted back to the buggy, as there were no improved roads in the county. Ten miles away, in Conway, South Carolina, the Atlantic Coast Railroad train came down Main Street. What a crowd was always there to see the passengers step off that "huge monster!" Living on a farm certainly had its advantages in so many ways. Children learned the facts of life being around animals and taking care of them.

Our cow Daisy showed up one morning with a beautiful little calf. We were entranced and spent practically the whole day atop the fence, just out of reach of old Daisy, who kept a watchful eye on us. The question that day was, "Where did she get that calf?" The best solution we could come up with was, "She stole it!" The thing that puzzled us was that our parents didn't seem surprised or puzzled.

We were still atop the fence at sundown, waiting for our Dad to come home and explain about the new calf, as we knew he would tell the truth. He studied a minute and propped his foot up on the fence. We held our breath, our eyes square on Dad. "Sure, old Daisy found the little calf behind a hollow log down in the creek swamp." We were so shocked at his answer we almost toppled off the fence.

We kids went into a conference immediately and decided that if our Daisy could find a calf behind a hollow log – she being a cow–why couldn't we do the same thing?

Early the next morning, we slipped out behind the barn and into the swamp, excited over the prospects of bringing home a calf. We walked and walked, but found no hollow log and no baby calf. About that time, we heard Mama frantically calling us.

Our expedition brought results, however, for not long after that we received an elementary lesson concerning "the birds and bees." We were cautioned that such things were not discussed in public. The fact is, we just wanted to understand the logic of life. Life's not always logical. The wisdom of God cannot always be grasped by the mind of a man. Somewhere along life, we have to be content and trust His superior wisdom. Only then will life become logical and make sense.

Those were the "olden days" and today, at 83 years, I still enjoy visiting a farm, especially the barns. I have seen many marvelous sights in my lifetime, some that will stand for many generations; others that are no longer standing.

Yes, today I can close my eyes and be a little girl again, cherishing memories which have helped me to survive. Yes, and to share some of my experiences with my grandchildren.

Lakota

Jeanette Levey
Alexian Village of Tennessee
Signal Mountain

Lakota, North Dakota, was a "city" of 900 residents in 1924 – a "city" because it was a county seat and most of the towns were made up of less than 300 people. My family embarked on a 2,000-mile drive to New York City in a brand new Studebaker sedan. This navy blue car had blue plush upholstery and vases for flowers; however, we had to convince my mother that it was safe to drive surrounded by glass windows instead of isinglass curtains. After having a key made for the front door which had never been locked and stowing clothes for five people for a month's trip, we took off. A new world opened up that day.

At twelve years of age, I had never seen street cars, els, elevators, escalators or buildings over two stories high, to say nothing of skyscrapers, hard surface highways, traffic cops, etc.

OUR MEMORIES

After stops in Milwaukee and Chicago to meet and visit relatives I had never seen, I thought I had been introduced to big city life; and in a sense, I had. However, we drove from Chicago to Detroit and boarded a Great Lake steamship overnight to Buffalo. It was my first experience on a ship or even a dinghy. I thought it was the *Normandie*.

Niagara Falls was an experience in itself. Dad took the five of us on the *Maid of the Mist*, a tiny boat that maneuvered at the base of the roaring torrent. Most of the time I was hanging on to my dad. Then we went into the Cave of the Winds at the base of and behind the falls. All in all it was a never-to-be-forgotten afternoon.

We drove as far as Syracuse, New York, arriving there in the evening. Dad asked for the best hotel, and we hit the jackpot. The Syracuse Hotel opened that night, and the celebration was in high gear. The women were in evening gowns and Spanish shawls, the men in tuxedoes. I thought I was in Hollywood. Little did I know I would spend 58 years in that city.

One more day to White Plains to visit dad's sister and her family. There I saw things I had never seen before and my 12-year-old cousin made the most of giving his country cousin misinformation about New York City. For instance, he told me sneakers had metal toes in the East and I should shop for a pair. (When he came to Lakota, we returned the teasing in spades; he had never seen a cow.) In Lakota we had had indoor plumbing for about five months, so when my mother sent me into the elegant bathroom to shower, I had no idea how to manipulate the controls. So I just splashed water on myself in the wash basin and never did take a shower for the whole week we were there.

New York City itself was frightening to me. When I walked between the skyscrapers the first time, I was sure they were closing down on me. Even today I can feel that sensation if I look up between their towers. We saw a play, a musical, went to a concert, and to an amusement park called Rye Beach, I think.

The drive home was uneventful, I am happy to say. It is remarkable that my father was able to do all the driving. There were no turnpikes until we got to the beautiful Taconic Parkway through Westchester County. This trip was the highlight of my adolescence, and the experiences are as vivid to me as they were in 1924. In fact, I take that trip frequently just before I go to sleep.

A River Outing
Helen Potts
Morningside of Franklin
Franklin

I have always lived near the Harpeth River, so I feel a sort of attachment to it. In my mind I can visualize the old covered bridge that was washed away in the flood of 1945. However, this was a second replacement, because the first was burned during the Civil War to keep the Union Army from crossing. The present bridge is a concrete structure.

The river was only a short distance from our home. And it always seemed

ROCK OF AGES

to call us, as children, to come and play. We were not permitted to go by ourselves, but only when father would go with us. Dressed in some old clothes (we had no bathing suits then) we were on our way to the river, where we splashed and played as long as he would stay with us.

An added attraction was a large sand bar where we hunted mussel shells and periwinkles. These skills brought on a lesson in science. Where did they come from? We learned that this area of Tennessee was once covered by water. This was in the antediluvian period and the periwinkle shells were left by this long ago water coverage. We do have mussels today, but not periwinkles. We collected shells to carry back and decorate dollhouses.

These were fun times that I like to remember.

A Story
Dorothy Morris
Alexian Brothers Valley Residence
Chattanooga

I met a man on an airplane who had a seeing eye dog. The dog was just shivering. I asked the man if I could just sit down on the floor and talk to his dog. He was a German shepherd. That dog stayed with me the whole time on the airplane. Animals have always liked me.

One day, a long time later, I was at the Continental. Some man was coming to speak to our group. I was a little late and when I walked in the door, this creature jumped off the stage and came running. He threw his paws up on my shoulders and greeted me. He didn't hurt me. I was just surprised that he remembered me.

You know, animals have a sense of people who enjoy them and are good to them. They just take to them, and I'm just one of them.

Memories of Life on the Farm...and Beyond
Irene Berry
Christian Towers and The Manor of Gallatin
Gallatin

I was born on a farm in Sumner County, Tennessee, the daughter of a hard working farmer who worked from sun up to sun down in the corn and tobacco fields. I had to quit school before I finished the sixth grade in order to help my sister and dad on the farm. Many were the mornings when my sister and I would get up before daylight and go to the barn to hitch the mule to the wagon, getting ready for the day's work. Then we'd go back to the house for breakfast. We each made $1.00 a day for working in those fields. Yes, life on the farm was hard, hard work, especially for a little girl.

A few years went by and my sister left home and went to Chicago to find work. About a year later, when I was seventeen, I decided that I had had all the farm life I could stand and went to my sister's in Chicago. In 1951 I got my first job in a factory in Chicago where I packed one piece sun visors. I made $.65 an hour and thought I was rich. My sister and I both sent money home to help support our family who were still laboring on the farm from sun up to sun down.

Years went by, and one day I met a wonderful man. We married and a year later our daughter was born. Times were great, but after eighteen years of marriage my husband passed away. Times got hard again, but with God's help my daughter and I survived. I worked two jobs in order to make ends meet. My daughter worked her way through medical school and became a registered nurse. She married a wonderful doctor and has been married for twenty-seven years.

Although I have not been blessed by having a grandchild, I accept the fact that it simply was not God's will. I have been blessed as I have grown older and retired. I was able to return to Sumner Country to be near my family that I had left behind. I have a good church, and I am able to serve as a volunteer at the local hospital. I live at a wonderful place called the Manor. I am happy again.

Mountains and Fried Chicken
Lalise M. O'Brien
McKendree Village
Hermitage

One of my great memories is our first visit to North Carolina. It probably occurred during the summer that I became five. We went on the train, and that was exciting. I'd ridden the train to go across Lake Pontchartrain from New Orleans, but I hadn't been on the train to spend the night since I'd been a baby, so it was very exciting to have a drawing room. My brothers, Dan and Brownie, were in the upper berth, and I was in the lower because the adults were afraid I would roll out of the top. We also had a little dressing room with a basin and a toilet. My mother and a friend who was accompanying us had the two lower berths right outside the drawing room.

The main thing I remember about the trip was that we had ice cream one time. The train would stop at places, and people could jump off and get things to eat. We got ice cream, and I remember that there were not enough utensils to eat with, so my mother washed off a shoe horn very carefully with hot water and soap, and I ate with the shoe horn. It was great fun.

Mother told us that in the morning we would be in the mountains. Oh! we were so excited! We'd already had a whole day on the train. We went to bed, and before he went to sleep, Brownie told me, "Now I'll come down early in the morning and wake you, and we can open the shades of the lower berth and look out." The upper berth had no windows. He said, "We can look out and see the mountains, and we'll be the first to see them." Well, that was fine with me. Sure enough, we all went to sleep, and next thing I knew Brownie was shaking me on the shoulders. Quietly he crept in, and each of us knelt by one of the two windows onto the lower berth. We took hold of the little things that you pressed to raise the shade, and he pressed his and I pressed mine. He said, "One, two, three, up!" and we raised 'em, looked out the window, and there was nothing there but the side of a cutoff. So, that was a big disappointment. We both said, "Ohhhh!" and leaned back, but suddenly we came out

ROCK OF AGES

of the cut-off and we could see the mountains in the distance, so our excitement increased, of course.

When we reached North Carolina, we went, probably in a big touring car, from the train to Mrs. Candler's Boarding House in Candler, North Carolina. Mrs. Candler was an ample lady who served wonderful meals and had a large frame house on the top of a hill where she took boarders. I don't know how high the hill was; I don't suppose it was very high. It was covered with daisies, and we thought it was heaven. It was a wonderful place to be.

Mrs. Candler had a lot of chickens. She would go out with a pan of chicken feed on Sunday mornings and other times during the week, and she would call the chickens. "Chick, chick, chick, chick!" Then she'd throw down the chicken feed, and we'd all come running because we knew what was going to happen. She would let the chickens eat the feed while she examined them and decided which one she wanted to snatch. Then she would grab one, and I don't know how she was holding it, but she spun it around and wrung its neck. Then she would toss it from her, and it would flop all over the place until it died thoroughly. It was dead already, I know, but there was a reflex of the muscles. We would stand and watch with gruesome, gruesome delight. Remember now, we had no TV, we had very few movies, and we certainly were not allowed to go to any (I doubt there were any) that had the violence and the slaughter they have nowadays. The chicken killing may have been sort of an outlet for us. I don't know, but we were fascinated when Mrs. Candler was catching the chickens for meals. It made no difference that the chicken we had seen having its neck wrung and jumping around in the reflex afterwards would appear on the table as the most delightful fried chicken you ever had. That would make no difference to us; we enjoyed it both times.

Mrs. Candler would also churn the milk and make the butter. She had a large churn that was like a barrel on its side, and she would sit and turn the handle at one end, and you could hear the milk flopping inside until finally it got too hard to flop. She would usually give us a drink of buttermilk before it got to the point of butter. So that was fun, too, to watch and listen to.

We took one trip while I was there; all the boarding house went. We had automobiles – large, open touring cars. In one there were all the little girls and Mrs. Candler. I don't know whether we had all the ladies in that car or not, but we had a female group. Mrs. Candler would tell us about the sights on the trip. The next thing we knew, we were up above the clouds; we could look down and see the clouds, and that was very exciting. On the way to Chimney Rock, we would stop and Mrs. Candler would say, "Anybody needs to make a little crick, come with me." And we would get out and walk with Mrs. Candler to a sort of secluded spot where everybody would "make a little crick," and then we'd walk back to the car feeling very much better and go on to where we could walk across to Chimney Rock. There we could see oh! wonderful views all below us. I have a picture of all of us at Chimney Rock. I'm there with a big bow in my hair. We had to wait 'til the sun came out, and in the picture Brownie is y-a-w-n-i-n-g; he was yawning just as they took the picture, so there he is with one arm on Mother's knee, yawning his head away.

OUR MEMORIES

The Roaring Twenties
Bruce Monroe
Alexian Village of Tennessee
Signal Mountain

It was an exciting period in American history, for the World War (one) was thought to be the war to "end all wars," and the economic prosperity of the U.S.A. was touted as "never ending." The Prohibition amendment lasted through the decade of the 20's and engendered widespread disrespect for the law. Violent gangster rule existed in all the large cities, and sociological turmoil involving the church and the changing mores of the 20's was present. Many of these changes influenced life throughout the U.S.A. for the rest of the entire century.

In a few years, just prior to the Great Depression of the 30's, there had been a fantastic creation of dozens of different makes of automobiles, for the automobile had become King. Railroads, very active for passenger transportation in even the very small towns of America for 30 years or more, were yielding rapidly to the automobile. The horse-buggy era, present throughout the world for centuries, was going, going, gone in about ten years!

The rapidity of the changes listed above have never been equaled in this century. The "Roaring Twenties" decade is generally acknowledged to have ended with the stock market crash in October, 1929. The Great Depression was under way. My personal story in this manuscript serves as a colorful base to depict rural culture here in the U.S.A. just about at the beginning of six years of the frenzied activities of the late twenties.

The setting for my tale is in the mid-summer of 1924, in rural northern Michigan. At that time it was a common practice for the whole family to go for a "Sunday drive" out into the countryside. I always looked forward to this drive, possibly because of intermittent interaction with my packed-in older siblings, and certainly because of the eventual ritual of opening the picnic basket that Mother had prepared, to be consumed at some lakeside cleared area after a refreshing swim.

Besides the above-mentioned items, much of the basic allure of these auto trips for me had to be a change of scenery. Obviously, in 1924, I had no TV distractions, much less computer games or e-mail. Sometimes, on Sunday afternoons, I would ride with my father and brothers to the small town nearby to watch a spirited baseball game, with accompanying accordion intermissions. I also had access to battery powered, post-embryonic squeaky radio programs. If the weather precluded an auto trip, a hand-wound Victrola would play 78 r.p.m. records, although not acoustically pleasant with their hand-sharpened wooden needles. You can readily see that I considered a Sunday drive in the country a magnificent event!

I know that my Dad also looked forward to these Sunday outings. Having just completed the standard 6-day work week, he would enjoy the pristine beauty of northern Michigan and at the same time have the opportunity to drive the 1922 Buick "touring car" of which he was immensely proud. Although the car was two years old, it must have appeared virtually new, for Dad had followed the manufacturer's recommendation that the car be supported on blocks (to preserve the tires) throughout the long Michigan winters. Incidentally, if we were out on a drive and rain showers arose, flexible isinglass curtains were hastily snapped into place where door windows are now standard. At best, the curtains kept out only some of the rain, but we kids did

ROCK OF AGES

not seem to mind.

While this Sunday trip was going on, our family horse, Jim, was grazing peacefully in the pastures, knowing that he would not be called on to pull the heavy buggy into town or to pull the buckboard for routine activities in our rural neighborhood. In the winter, of course, he would be called on to pull the sleigh (jingle bells and all!) into town and to pull a plow for planting in the spring. Such a sleigh ride was absolutely delightful! Since no picnic lunch was involved, for me at least, it had to take a close second place behind the summer Sunday outing.

One day, in the mid-summer of 1923, while returning from such a picnic trip, Dad applied the brakes with determination, causing the car to swerve and skid on the gravel highway US-2. The mechanical brakes, rear wheels only, soon brought the vehicle to a stop, and by this time we were all very alert. Dad urgently got us all out of the car, traffic not being a problem for there was no other car to be seen. Following his animated directions we looked to the sky to see what he had seen through the two-piece windshield. It was an airplane, the very first one seen by any of us. Dad had read about it, so he knew that it was a Ford Trimotor plane, used only by Ford management to transport their officials from Detroit to a newly opened factory in northern Michigan which manufactured wooden spokes and other wooden parts for Ford Model T's.

When the initial excitement had subsided, Dad clearly prophesied that we would all remember this scene. How very true! In just three short years Lindbergh would fly from the U.S.A. to France non-stop, and world-wide isolationism was viewing its eventual demise. Here at home, from humble beginnings in the "Roaring Twenties," the Automobile and the Airplane dominated transportation for the remaining 70 years of the 20th century, and many remnants of the sociological changes mentioned in my opening paragraph have remained with us to this day.

My Aunt Bessie

Joanne Smalling
Sycamores Terrace Retirement Community
Nashville

Aunt Bessie was a survivor – way before the ERA or the women's movement. Left penniless by an irresponsible husband, she did what she could to feed herself and her two boys. Barely able to read or write, Bessie's only skills were those gained by growing up in a country household of seven siblings. She knew how to scrub floors, wash clothes on a scrub board, and iron them with a flat iron heated on a coal stove. So that's what she did in our small town for whoever would hire her.

Washing for people back then meant having two tin tubs with a fire under the wash tub and a rinse tub that often froze in winter. No one ever let her into their homes to warm up in the winter or offered her a cool drink in the summertime. But Aunt Bessie kept a sharp eye out to better herself and got a job cleaning the local hotel, and that led to what she thought was an even better job: she became the cook at the hotel, three meals a day, but she could take home the leftovers for the boys. Up 'til this point, this was the best they had ever had. But then disaster hit Aunt Bessie when the hotel closed. She managed by the skin of her teeth. A man who owned a market offered her a job in his market, which she jumped at, but there was one big problem: she had been evicted from the rooms she was living in.

The man who owned the market told her if she could clean an old building he owned, she could live there rent free. It had not been used in years and had never been used for anything but a meat market. Aunt Bessie cleaned it up and lived in those two rooms with an outhouse for many years. It was at this time that she started cooking for any occasion for all the family, and she could really cook! No one could beat her in the kitchen! The signs were there, even then, of what would happen in the coming years, but no one saw it. Back then, she saved every newspaper that was sold at the market and brought them home and stacked them in a corner. She also collected fruit jars and tin cans.

Aunt Bessie lived in poverty. But she always went to church, and if there was a "meeting" and someone asked her to go, she was always ready. Her boys were grown by then – the oldest was in the army – and she got money from them. She saved every penny she could, and with help from my father, she bought lumber to build a house. When the men brought the lumber, they dumped it in a ditch, so I helped for four days to get the lumber moved to where the house was to be built. When she saw the lumber, she began wringing her hands and saying, "Oh, sweet Jesus."

Aunt Bessie's house was built way before Habitat for Humanity was dreamed up. She worked on it, one son who was in high school worked on it, and many other people worked on it until it was finished. Just as the house was nearing completion, her elder son was discharged from the Army, came home, and was in on the completion of the house. The house was perfectly square. There was a large kitchen, and since the boys were both at home, there was a large bedroom for them. The other two rooms were a living room and Aunt Bessie's bedroom. The house was only about 40' x 40', but it was like heaven to her. Looking back on moving day is a scream: she moved that huge stack of papers, the fruit jars, the tin cans, and "Oh, sweet Jesus" with her.

Aunt Bessie was so proud that she had a sink with running water. This was the first time she had ever had water in the house that she didn't have to carry. Of course, it was a given that they had an outside backhouse. Aunt Bessie lived in her dream house for several years. Then at church one day she met Mr. Wright; she thought of him as "rich Mr. Right." They courted for a few months and then lo and behold they married. Aunt Bessie never spent another night in her dream house.

They moved her many, many belongings, including her huge amount of newspapers, fruit jars, and tin cans, to Mr. Wright's house in a nearby town. The boys were happy that she now had someone to look after her. Back then, women got older than they do now, or maybe they thought they must have a man in the house to make all the decisions. Aunt Bessie didn't like the house they moved into. She seemed to connect land with money, so they soon moved into a much bigger house on a small farm. And that was heaven for her. She filled two bedrooms with her newspapers. Since Mr. Wright would take her to the biggest stores she had ever seen, and she bought groceries, she bought everything in sight. Aunt Bessie filled the house, the root cellar, a closed-in back porch, and a small storehouse with food and newspapers. At any time you could find four or five cakes and pies on the beds. She was truly happy there, and so was Mr. Wright. He allowed her to buy anything to add to her store. Mr. Wright was a lot older than Aunt Bessie, but nobody had the nerve to mention it. One day Mr. Wright had a car wreck and ended up in the hospital. His three children, who had never been around, came in and took over. Mr. Wright lived only a few days. The Wright children made all the arrangements and Aunt Bessie's boys were fit to be tied. Every time they started to say something, Aunt Bessie just would wring her hands and say, "Oh, sweet Jesus, Mr. Wright's children will do right by me."

The Wright family took care of Aunt Bessie, and the word is "took." They sold the farm and "bought" Aunt Bessie a tiny house on a heavily traveled country road. The house was right on the road, but there was a garage and driveway that made it easier to get into the house. Aunt Bessie somehow found some huge rocks and blocked the driveway. She said she didn't want any car in her yard. The Wright family brought all her newspapers, fruit jars, and tin cans. After finding those rocks, she stayed in that house with the shades down for thirty years, never going further than the front door. Every time anyone went to see her, she would start wringing her hands and saying, "Oh, sweet Jesus." Every year the house got dirtier, smelled worse, and so did Aunt Bessie. Every time her sons sent someone to clean, she ran them off with a broom handle she kept by her chair. Her sons finally said, "To hell with it," and sent her granddaughter to give her a bath so they could taker her to the brand new double wide they had placed next to one of her sons' trailer. The boys caught her by surprise.

They went in and said, "Mom, you are moving right now," and, as always, she started wringing her hands and said, "Oh, sweet Jesus, I can't move. I don't have anything packed. Oh, sweet Jesus, maybe after the first of the month. Oh, sweet Jesus, what am I going to do?"

They took her by the arm and had to drag her to the car. All the way she was doing the "sweet Jesus" thing and asking for them to be sure and bring her newspapers when they brought her things because there were things in them she wanted to read. Was she surprised when she walked into that spanking new trailer and the second bath of the day! But she is clean, the newspapers, the fruit jars and the tin cans are gone, and the trailer is clean, there is no dirt around. If you listen you can hear Aunt Bessie saying, "Oh, sweet Jesus."

A "Greenhorn" Celebrates Ninety Years in the USA
Helen Baker Muccio
Jamestowne Assisted Living Community
Kingston

It was 1908 and I was six years old when my parents and I left Budapest for New York. Left behind was my Lizzie, who had taken care of me since birth. Early every morning she and I would go to St. Stephen's Church where at the font we would dip our hands in the holy water and walk in. There the priest would give her and me a white wafer.

The house we lived in had a big courtyard at the front of which were gates and a small building in which a man sat. I guess you had to prove that you lived there or knew somebody there. Inside the courtyard were stairs on either side that led up to a balcony onto which all the apartments opened.

OUR MEMORIES

We left Budapest for Hamburg, where we embarked on the *S.S. Bremen* in May of 1908 for New York. There we would meet Mama's mother, Mama's two sisters, and my two boy cousins. There were lots of children on the boat. I think most of the people on the boat were coming to the States to stay. There were people from Czechoslovakia, Hungary, but mostly Germany.

Mama was sick almost the entire trip, but my father and I were fine, so we were on the deck every day and I saw and learned many things. One day, Papa pointed to a little dot off in the distance behind the ship. He said, "That little dot is a ship, a big ship. As we watch it every day, it will get bigger and bigger." And, sure enough, a few days later it was ahead of us and finally it disappeared. Papa learned from the seamen that it was the famous *S.S. Kaiser Wilhelm*. It reached New York about three or four days earlier than we did. Our *Bremen* was a very old ship that had lost an important screw. That malfunction slowed the ship considerably.

After some days, my father pointed out something. He said, "Honka! Birds! Do you know what that means? That means we're near land!" (My name was Ilona, but sometimes he called me "Honka." When they add the "-ka" in Hungarian it's like an endearment.) "Honka! Look! That means we're near land." Soon we were docking.

Ellis Island! As we got off the boat we were directed to a very large room where we were required to report. It had many desks with a man sitting at each and a doctor. The men at the desks were checking documents. The doctor examined the eyes particularly. He was looking for the eye disease trachoma, a serious contagious disease. Those with trachoma were not allowed to enter the United States. My mother was very worried about my eyes because they were red due to the salt water. She said, "I hope we don't have to go back after all this!" Of course, we were okay and passed through. I pointed out to my father that the houses all had flat roofs whereas in Hungary the roofs had been slanted and gabled. The flatness of the buildings was my first impression of America. Then we saw our relatives.

There was much hugging and kissing, and finally my aunts hailed a horse and buggy, which in Hungary we called a *fiacre*. We arrived at our new home on Second Street on the Lower East Side where our relatives had an apartment ready for us. My parents looked somewhat heartsick. They had left an apartment in a stone and brick building, clean and attractive, and here we were in a dirty, smelling, three-story wooden building which was very dilapidated. Of course, my parents concealed their disappointment.

My aunts had prepared much good food, and my two boy cousins brought in a big heavy stalk with yellow fruit on it which they urged me to eat. It was so sweet I could not eat much of it. I hated it. Now I can't eat enough of it! We had never had bananas in Budapest!

This is how I met my grandmother, my Aunt Malvina, and my Aunt Sophie. Aunt Sophie and Uncle Armin had come from Baltimore to be with us. Aunt Sophie and Armin had come to New York in 1890. Aunt Malvina, the boys, and Grandmother came in 1892 after the terrible loss of my Uncle Tobias, my grandmother's youngest child, who died of pneumonia at age 32. He was the youngest Supreme Court Justice and the first Jew ever appointed to that high office in Hungary.

My father was a color pressman – a printer who specialized in color printing. When we came here to the United States, he wanted to work immediately. He got the German paper *Zeitung* and found the ad, applied, and was hired the very same day.

So we settled into our apartment on Second Street where we had two

ROCK OF AGES

rooms. One was a bedroom, very small, for my parents. Then there was the kitchen, which had a gas range for cooking and an iron-bellied stove for heating; close beyond that was a couch on which I slept. Also, there was a table and four chairs and a dresser in which my mother kept linens and utensils. We lived there until I was seventeen years old, when I graduated from high school, obtained a job as a secretary and began earning a salary.

As sparsely and uncomfortably as we lived, my mother made the place look and feel as comfortable as possible. She made by hand lovely starched white curtains, she always kept the place spotless and clean, and her wonderful Hungarian meals kept us well.

There was an incident I'll never forget that happened a day or so after we arrived. Before we left Budapest, my Aunt Marie, who sewed and crocheted beautiful laces, had made me a lovely navy blue serge cape lined in red, with a hood. I had gone to the top step to the stoop of our house to look around outside, wearing my lovely cape. Suddenly, at the foot of the stairs there were boys and girls yelling and shouting, "Greenhorn! Greenhorn!" I ran back into the house crying, not daring to go out for days.

Finally, it was school time. I was registered as Helen rather than Ilona; I am not sure who made the decision to change my name or why. I was seven in July, so I was placed in the second grade where I met my very close and lifelong friend Tilly. We were friends for 75 years. She died at 82 years of age.

My teacher was Miss Quartlander, who seemed very anxious to get me to talk, but I was scared and very shy. She tried to find out what language I spoke, to no avail. Finally, she lifted me onto her desk and talked and questioned but got little response. Then she noticed lace peeking from below my skirt. She was impressed with the lace made by my Aunt Marie – or Mari Neni ("neni" means aunt) – and I finally opened up somewhat. I attempted to tell her all about the beautiful cape Aunt Marie had made me, as well as the beautiful laces on my clothes, but she didn't understand Hungarian.

My mother and father spoke Hungarian to me and German to each other when they didn't want me to understand. But when I began to understand, they were out of luck! After they had been in the States awhile, they learned to speak English. My mother mostly spoke Hungarian. So I know a bit of German, Hungarian, Yiddish, Spanish, and English.

I have to backtrack to mention happenings I feel are of interest, like the fire in the next house which brought the fire truck pulled by two horses with Dalmatians running alongside.

One day we heard a big band from a distance, coming closer and closer, then finally we saw marchers. In the center, surrounded by many other men, was a heavy-set man dressed in Rough Rider clothes, with a big hat that he raised to the watching crowd. It was Theodore Roosevelt, electioneering for President.

Sunday was my outing day with my father. My father was very well read and would tell me about Jules Verne's book about how someday ships would travel under the sea. I learned a lot from him. Often on Sundays we would go by the way of the First Avenue elevated train to Battery Park to the Aquarium or take the ferry to Staten Island; on the way we would see the Statue of Liberty.

On one occasion when we were ready to get off the train, I had gotten off but my father was sandwiched between two men who would not let him pass when the conductor was ready to close the door. I yelled and cried and finally the conductor opened the door and my father stepped out. My father pulled out a crumpled paper from his pocket and laughed and laughed. It seems those men holding him were pickpockets but all they got were my baby teeth in his wallet. His money was in a crumpled piece of paper.

There was a happening every night that I never wanted to miss.

Especially in the fall and winter I would stand on my stoop around 4:00 p.m. when it would start to darken and wait for the lamplighter. Sure enough he would come with his long pole and touch each streetlamp with his stick. I never wanted to miss him.

At this writing I am 98 years old. As through a kaleidoscope I see my life evolve with happiness and sorrow, but with gratitude for the privilege and fortune to have lived and grown old in this country.

My First Day of School
James Cornelius Hundley
McKendree Village
Hermitage

My first day at school was unforgettable. My Dad, whom I adored and would do anything to please, took me for my first day. I carried with me a bat, ball, glove, a pencil and a tablet. The latter two were incidentals as far as I was concerned. I had never been so shocked as when I heard my Dad tell the teacher he would back her 100% and if she found it necessary to punish me to let him know and he would also punish me when I came home. This coming from a Dad who, up to this point, had never so much as spanked me. I guess I was just about as good as could be! At least I think he felt that way. Now it is quite a different matter with my somewhat Irish Mother. She had the most sensitive sense of smell of anyone. When I walked in the front door she could smell if I had been smoking and her all the way back in the kitchen. She did a rather thorough job with her switching. I didn't once ask for more.

In the first or second grade it was considered a privilege to get to take the erasers out and knock the chalk out until they were clean. Well, I got to do this; then, to be more helpful, I asked the teacher if I could clean out her drawers. I couldn't understand why she and her boyfriend, who happened to be there, burst out laughing.

My Long Lost First Love
Irene Berry
Christian Towers and The Manor of Gallatin
Gallatin

I remember the days as a teenager, living in Chicago with my sister. I was making $ .65 an hour and sending part of it back home to help support my family. Wow, I was making big money!

I met and fell in love with a young man, my first LOVE! However, as time went on we parted ways. He went his way and I went mine. I guess we both thought we wanted to explore the world, without each other.

I later married another fine man, however, never forgetting my first love. After eighteen years of married life and the birth of a wonderful daughter, my husband, whom I loved, passed away, leaving us alone. After I had begun to get over the sadness of losing my husband, I began to try to find my "first love" only to be told that he too had passed away. Sadness filled my heart again thinking that I would never see him again.

Forty-eight years went by and many changes took place in the world. One day in 1998 my sister called and said that she had found the address of my "first love" on the computer. He was now living in Texas. I got his address and phone number and could hardly wait to give him a call. My heart was again filled with excitement having found my "first love." He too was excited to hear from me. His wife had also died, and he was now living alone. He would call at least once a week and most of the time twice a week. We sent each other pictures. He even had a picture of the two of us taken years ago when we dated. Plans were made for us to again get together in the spring of 2000 after a year and a half of corresponding with each other. But it wasn't to be. My "first love" passed away in January, 2000, never to be seen by me on this earth again. He is with Jesus now, and I know that we will see each other again in heaven when this life is over.

My lost love was found, and lost again, but not forever!!

The Bear and I
Faith Cornwall
McKendree Village
Hermitage

It was a warm, sunny day in Yellowstone National Park. My family and I were making a leisurely trip through the park on our way to Florida from Idaho. Since we were contemplating making Florida our home, our Model T Ford was loaded with luggage and people. Three in the front seat and three in the back were my parents, my brother age 9, myself age 7, and two grandparents who were "old." On the floor of the back seat was a large bag of apples from our reliable backyard tree.

We had watched with awe as Old Faithful performed on schedule. Now we had come to a wooded area where we thought we would likely see bears.

Surely enough, we did see one not much larger than a big dog, too small to put fear into the heart of a seven year old lover of dogs.

Excited, I flung open the door of the car and ran to greet him. My grandmother, sensing the danger, grabbed an apple and ran after me.

"Stop," she cried. I replied, "He's a nice bear! If you treat him nice, he'll treat you nice."

Thinking to distract the bear, she threw the apple to him, but her aim was too good. She hit him squarely on the nose! This seemed to anger the bear, and he quickened his pace toward us.

By this time, I recognized the danger myself, and turned and ran as fast as my little legs would carry me, my grandmother running closely behind. We scrambled into the car and slammed the door. My father revved up the motor and we sped

OUR MEMORIES

away, leaving the bewildered bear behind.

Since then, I have visited other national parks and have seen other bears. But never again have I tested my theory that if you treat a bear nice, he'll treat you nice. Nevertheless, in my long life (I am 82), I have many times experienced the kernel of truth in that childhood philosophy, that the kindnesses you extend to people and creatures will inevitably, in their own time, return to you.

Old Do-It-Yourselfers Never Die, They Just Roll Off the Roof

Mardelle S. Bourdon
Uplands Retirement Village
Pleasant Hill

Mamma warned me about marrying a crafty man! She believed barbers' children always need haircuts and shoemakers' children go barefoot. Once, she predicted I would find myself living along the river in a packing crate if I dare marry a man with a hammer in his pocket. I knew she was wrong as soon as I saw Jim. He could make anything. What could be better than a man who could keep me in enough closets and shelves?

There were surprises along the way, all right, and they could have upset me were I not so deeply in love. It was those "birds-of-a-feather" pals that made life interesting. Jack, "wood carver supreme," had a philosophy declaring if one had skills enough to make beautiful things, he would spend his life doing just that. Dumb yokels who could do nothing creative would get lucrative jobs and would hire people with talents. It worked that way for him. He never brought home a full paycheck.

There was a dear old Swede named Ercy who measured the woodwork of his wedding suite instead of admiring Marge as she emerged from the dressing room in bridal finery. "Would you believe this door frame is off a whole half inch," he queried as he stretched out his tape measure. Bill, another genius, took two old bicycles and a broken dining room table to create a mobile sleeping-dining room cabin. His children refused to ride in the same ferry with him, and he couldn't understand their reluctance. But the rest of us did!

This started from the "git-go" with Jim. I know a man's home is his castle, but I was more than a little surprised when he bought a house with a basement full of water. He intended to build a stairway to our indoor swimming pool, but it became easier to sell the house. When carrying out three buckets of water for every one we carried in that mansion became a chore, he took up the plumber's trade. It was so much fun, he wanted a bigger challenge as soon as the house became livable. Yes, I was dismayed when he bought an eight-apartment affair, called "Cockroach Place" by the neighbors. But, I lived through it.

It's the geriatric "do-it-yourselfer" who has me whipped. Retirement seems to provide only more hours for living dangerously. His days are spent pounding nails and sawing boards. The bird feeders wear shields made of furnace metal and our ceramic tiles are grouted with plaster mixed in my $49 roaster. (I wasn't very nice about that one.) Now, my friend Pat has come with a picture, taken while I was away. There they are, big as life: Jim, our son Bill, and Bill's son Christopher! Three generations up on the roof! The legacy of "do-it-yourselfers" goes on...and on...and on...

ROCK OF AGES

The Sweet Pits
Lester A. Ludlow
McKendree Village
Hermitage

I was a young boy living what I felt was a normal life. I have a brother two years older than I, and we were always around the neighborhood keeping our hands on everything.

At the back of our house was a garden which we hated to hoe and water. Along the back of the garden were a fence and a chicken coop. At the side of the coop was a screen, approximately 6 ft. x 8 ft., to let a cool breeze into the coop to cool it off in the summertime.

The side of the fence faced the neighbor's lot; in fact, it was on the property line. Well, right there on the neighbor's property was a large apricot tree loaded with apricots. It was known that the pits were sweet, so here we had a whole tree for the taking.

It didn't take long to peel off the apricot and put the pits in a bag, more nuts than we'd get for Christmas. We found a place on the pavement to crack the nuts, and we began to eat them.

Just as we were going full blast, the lady who owned the tree asked us why we were cracking them in front of her walk. She also wanted to know where we got the nuts and what we did with the fruit. We told her that we just left it. She insisted that she had to inspect the area where we left the fruit. Well, all the apricots were scattered on the ground. The neighbor was very upset about the wasted fruit, so she gave us strict instructions to go back and eat the fruit. After we ate the fruit, we were to let her know so that she could inspect the area.

My brother and I began eating the fruit, and it didn't take long before we were both stuffed. Inadvertently, one of us put an apricot against the screen of the coop and a chicken plucked it. We threw one inside and the chickens fought over it. We knew then who was going to eat the fruit. We pushed the fruit through to the chickens and they cleaned it up. We got the lady, and we passed inspection. We were relieved that she didn't observe all the chickens lining up on the other side of the screen as we approached.

Devoted Listening
Sara S. Shipley
Appalachian Christian Village at Sherwood
Johnson City

When you are the little sister of a clean, quiet, cooperative big brother, the easiest way to be noticed is to be obnoxious. So, I was frequently in trouble.

When I had gotten myself in a real mess, there was one escape: I would scoop up Tom, my cat, and retreat to my little blue room upstairs where I would pour out all my troubles to him. Tom never complained that I was keeping him from a lot of important mouse work he should be doing. He listened. He did not complain that my wet tears were messing up the coat he had just washed so carefully. He listened. He neither condemned nor condoned anything I had done. He just let me pour out all the details until I had sorted it all out and was ready to face the consequences. He listened in his compassionate way. The world is full of talkers. How I wish we had more devoted listeners.

Extending the Dinner Table
Marietta Dickerson
Alexian Village of Tennessee
Signal Mountain

The surgeon said he would use the kitchen table for my tonsillectomy! There was no way to do it in any hospital in Buffalo, because a strange epidemic was going across the country and only emergency patients were admitted. It was 1918. Doctors were just beginning to realize they were dealing with a new and serious illness. No nurse was available, but a young uncle, a good short-order cook, was asked to give the ether. The surgeon seemed to have confidence he could get those adenoids and tonsils out successfully in these primitive conditions! I was six years old, and the important memory of this was the promise that I could have ice cream when it was all over. Of course, as I awoke from the ether-sleep, I could care less about ice cream!

Before I had fully recovered, however, the flu epidemic took hold in our household. It was a frightening plague. No one knew just what to do. People wore a mask to cover their nose and mouth. The Buffalo newspaper had three pages of death notices in one day. Funeral directors were allowed to bury without embalming because of an overload of cases to care for.

A kind aunt came in from her farm home 30 miles away to help where she could, since all of our family was terribly sick. Remarkably, we all had a good recovery. My only problem was humiliation from having to sleep in the crib so that each patient could be isolated! The Board of Health had some very strict rules regarding diseases and enforced quarantine as if they were the police. In 1924 my Mother suspected I might have scarlet fever, and took me on the trolley car to the doctor's office. The trip needed a transfer to a second trolley. Sure enough, Mother was right, I did have scarlet fever. The return trip home meant two more trolley cars would have passengers exposed to my contagious disease.

Then the Board of Health representative arrived and nailed a yellow sign on our front door, quarantining everything inside. A blue card nailed to the door meant diphtheria, a white one meant whooping cough, while a red one was for German measles. Now the Board of Health enforced the quarantine. My sister stayed at the neighbor's house for six weeks. The sun-room which adjoined our dining room was sealed off with wide brown tape. My father lived there, coming to the back door for meals to be passed out to him. The Health Inspector would not remove the sign until my skin "peeled," a situation he thought indicated that I was no longer infectious. Children walking home from school crossed the street, when they saw me on the front porch at Halloween dressed as a witch and riding a broom. I was all better, but that yellow sign was still on the door.

By this time, I am sure mother had cabin fever, and so did I. A library book could not be returned until the house was fumigated and the sign removed. It was a happy day when our family of four could sit at the kitchen table together.

Terry's New Challenge
Ruth R. Broyles
Appalachian Christian Village at Sherwood
Johnson City

The school year had started smoothly. Schedules had worked out well with every student well situated.

A few weeks after school started, I saw two policemen coming around the front of the building accompanied by a young boy. They came to inform the school that Terry would be enrolling in our school because he would be living with a family in the school district.

Terry had not had the kind of life of an average boy. He had not spent a regular school year in his life. He had spent nights in any place he could find and had eaten food from garbage cans or did without.

Terry said he was twelve years old, although he did not have any school records to prove it. One of the fifth grade teachers volunteered to take Terry into her classroom. Terry did not trust anyone and watched the teacher every minute. I worked with Terry throughout the day to try to identify his interests. We tried very hard to show Terry that we really wanted to help him. We wanted desperately for him to trust us, and we felt it was important not to remind Terry of his past but to focus on the present and the future. Terry began to respond to our kindness and genuine concern for his well being.

Students from East Tennessee State University and Milligan College were available to assist our students with additional help in certain subjects. Terry took advantage of extra help. After a couple of months, Terry began to act like a normal boy. He finished the fifth and sixth grades in our school and went on to complete high school.

Years later, a well dressed young man walked in the school looking for me, as I was still principal at that time. He gave me a big hug and said, "If it had not been for you, I would never have been able to get this diploma."

Terry's story is a wonderful success, showing what can be accomplished in the lives of young people through kindness, love and encouragement.

A Humbling Experience
Bruce Monroe
Alexian Village of Tennessee
Signal Mountain

A recent news story reminded me of a personal episode which occurred many years ago when I was a resident in thoracic surgery in a charity hospital. On a particular morning for this tale, it was routine for our patients requiring bronchoscopies to be scheduled in the operating rooms as a group, one patient right after the other, interspersed with the usual clean-up and prep of the O.R. for each patient. As a resident chest surgeon, it was my role to insert a firm metal tube, called a bronchoscope, into the patient's windpipe, and then proceed to visualize the various branches thereof, all this being done under local anesthesia. At best, it was not very pleasant for the patient, depending in great measure on the skill of the operator. One must bear in mind that this was done with a firm metal instrument, not a flexible smaller diameter bronchoscope as is used today.

At one point, while awaiting the next patient, I engaged in light conversation with the man whom I had just completed. He was lying on a wheeled stretcher out in the hall, waiting transfer back to his room. He had been very quiet during the operative phase, and even now responded that he felt fine, with no complaints. He seemed to me to be a very polite elderly man, probably stoic throughout his lifetime. He asked me what was the name of the operation he had just had, and upon my response he asked me to spell it out. This elicited an additional request for me to please write it out.

Being somewhat proud of my imagined technical skill, I printed it out in large letters: BRONCHOSCOPY.

I even carefully pronounced the word, syllable by syllable. He accepted the paper, folded it neatly, and placed it in his robe pocket, and then stated firmly, "Thank you, Doctor, I'm going to keep this with me, 'cuz I ain't never going to sign for this again."

A Travel in Time

Gladys Gilliam Fillers
Appalachian Christian Village at Sherwood
Johnson City

One summer, my poppy, Charlie Gilliam, and my mother, Pearlie Rhodes Gilliam, set off on a travel with my brother Curtis and me in a real covered wagon. We started out in Pocahontas, Virginia, which is where I am originally from, and we headed to Kingsport, Tennessee.

The wagon we traveled in had stays that made arches over the back of the wagon that were covered with thick, white material called ducking material. The material had a string in it to tie up the end. It was a good cover that did not let any water in. The wagon was drawn by two horses and was driven by my poppy. In the back, we carried a few belongings and some provisions we needed for the trip. Also in the back of the wagon Poppy had put a mattress for us to sit on and sleep on.

During the travel, we would have to stop the wagon for the night to sleep. Whenever it was time to stop, Poppy would find out whose land we were on and ask them if it was all right for us to stay the night. All the farm people were always nice and would even let us turn out our horses in the fields. It was during these stops when mother would wash our clothes. She would go to a creek to wash and hang the clothes on a fence to dry. As mother did up the chores, Poppy would see if there was anything he could do to help on the farm where we stayed the night. Sometimes he would help put hay up and things like that.

ROCK OF AGES

When evening came, mother would build a fire and cook a big pot of soup beans. We would also have a skillet of fried potatoes and fried cornbread. In the mornings for breakfast, mother would fry some meat, fix gravy, fry wheat bread, and fix a big pot of coffee. We always ate good during our travel. If we would pass by an apple tree during the day's travel, Poppy would stop the wagon and climb up on the seat and pick some apples to eat

As we would drive along, sometimes Poppy would give us a song. I remember one of the songs he used to sing:

Put on your old gray bonnet
With the blue ribbons on it
While I hitch old Dobbin to the shay
We will all ride over to the Cliffs of Dover
On our golden wedding day!

During our travel my brother and I were young, and I do not remember many things about the journey. Many years later, my mother told me about one night when she awakened during a storm and felt for Poppy, but Poppy wasn't there. She then saw a streak of lightning and saw Poppy's shadow outside. He was outside holding the cover of the wagon together to keep the rain out. I do not know how long our travel took that summer, but when we reached Kingsport we stayed with relatives until we sold our wagon and horses. We then rode on a passenger train back to Pocahontas.

I started school when I was seven years old. My birthday is on Christmas Day, and back then you had to be a certain age to start school. So, I was always older then my classmates. I went on to graduate as salutatorian from Pocahontas High School in 1936. There were twelve students in my graduating class, and I still have the commencement speech that I gave during our graduation.

OUR MEMORIES

Reflecting on Reaching Age Ninety
Clara Anniss McCartt
Appalachian Christian Village at Sherwood
Johnson City

Next month, the Lord willing, I will celebrate my ninetieth birthday. Never would I have dreamed life could bring so much joy.

As a four-year-old, I trailed after my older siblings each morning as they started to school. Mother grew tired of that. She told us about it. The teacher said, "Let her come on; she'll get tired and drop out." I said to myself, "That teacher doesn't know what she's talking about. I'll never get tired of school." And, I never did.

During high school, I worked at part-time jobs. One Christmas, I noticed many of my customers were solemn-faced, so I smiled at them until they smiled back.

Graduation from high school came at age sixteen. Due to the Depression, formal college education was out. Later, I accumulated many college credits via night school.

My high school principal surprised me by recommending me for a secretarial job in a local firm. I had no particular desire to be a secretary, but a job was a job. That experience set me on a lifetime career. From that day until I retired at age 66, I was never without a job. My jobs have given me opportunity to travel to all the big cities of the United States, and to Canada, Mexico, South America, and Europe. Once I spent an entire year in Scotland.

Perhaps one reason I have been so fortunate is that I am an optimist, always eager to do what I could to help wherever I found myself. The Lord gives all of us some talent. If we sit back and never get involved, we wither and die on the vine, so to speak.

If we look on the bright side, things will get better. You know that before there is a rainbow, there must be clouds as well as sunshine. So let the sunshine into your life, and God's rainbow of promise will shine through on rainy days.

ROCK OF AGES

CHAPTER II

OUR SELVES

Meet some of the older adults who are part of the Tennessee's senior heritage. Their lives are a representation of the many older adults in our state whose work, love and life have made the world into the place we know today.

ROCK OF AGES

Biography: *Christine Lamb McMahon*
Integrated Health Services of Nashville
Nashville

Christine Lamb McMahon, born October 22, 1906, in Nashville, Tennessee, is 90 years young and has been a resident of IHS for eight years. She appreciates all the IHS employees who have shown so much affection and devotion to her.

Christine was educated at Hume Fogg High School, Ward Belmont College, and the Chicago Musical College through a scholarship. She had the gift of a beautiful natural contralto voice.

During the 1930s and 1940s, Christine was employed by the National Life & Accident Insurance Company as a librarian and as a singer for the famed Grand Ole Opry Radio Station WSM. She was a member of the Sacred Quartet, a program which aired over WSM each Sunday afternoon for many years.

Early in 1936 she was selected, along with George D. Hay, to represent National Life, WSM and the Grand Ole Opry at the Texas Centennial in Dallas. She met and married John McMahon during her stay there. Christine has a son, four grandchildren, and four great-grandchildren. She is a member of McKendree Methodist Church. During her active years, her hobbies were music and painting. Now she collects teddy bears and is an avid TV watcher.

Biography: *James Ozment*
Integrated Health Services of Nashville
Nashville

James Calvin Ozment, known to his friends as "Big Jim," was born August 16, 1916, in Dyersburg, Tennessee. He was raised on a farm, the youngest of six children and the only son. He married Evelyn Ozment of Newbern, Tennessee, and was happily married for over 50 years. They had two children, Sheila and Jim. He has one grandson and is awaiting the arrival of a granddaughter.

During his working years, Jim worked as a farmer, worked for the Illinois Central Railroad, sold insurance, managed a restaurant and even worked as a cook on a towboat on the Mississippi River. He is happiest when around people and always enjoyed jobs dealing with the public. His jobs required him to move his family frequently, and he spent several years in California.

Jim's hobbies included hunting and fishing and just being outdoors. As any of you who know him know, his favorite hobbies today are talking, smoking and drinking coffee.

Jim has been a resident of IHS since May of 1996 and wants to express his appreciation to all the staff for their hard work, kindness and friendship.

OUR SELVES

Biography: *Willie Mae Brown*
Wesley Highland Towers
Memphis

Mrs. Willie Mae Brown represents so much to our family. She is a great-great-grandmother, great-grandmother, grandmother, daughter, sister, aunt, cousin to many and my Mother. Through her love, generosity, kindness, wisdom, strength and dedication to God, she has shaped a productive future for us all.

The memories of her past date back to 1845 in Haywood County (Brownsville, Tennessee). The 1860 census shows two North Carolina slave owners, James Bond and W.P. Bond, who settled in Brownsville, Tennessee, as being responsible for the large number of the Bonds in that area.

Willie Mae is the daughter of Charlie and Callie Bond. She was born July 3, 1898. She was the fourth born of 16 siblings. She and her sister Lucille Cowan are the only remaining children of that union. We celebrated her centennial "100th" birthday in Memphis, Tennessee, on the weekend of July 3, 1998. She was surrounded by relatives and loved ones from around the country. Our "Rock of Ages" received warm wishes from public officials that included Mayor Willie Herenton, Senator John Ford, and President and Mrs. Bill Clinton.

Willie Mae is the Mother of five children. In birth order, we are Mary McKay of Los Angeles, California; Eula Garner (deceased) of Chicago, Illinois; Georgia Bell of Indianapolis, Indiana; Ned Taylor (deceased) and Opal Carpenter-Mayfield of Memphis, Tennessee.

Mother's vision for our future remains a work in progress. She serves as a constant role model. She is a faithful Christian servant at the New Friendship Missionary Baptist Church where she served as an usher for over 60 years. Her command of the English language has inspired us all to be lifelong learners. Even now at the age of 102, she reads the newspaper. Her professional life includes culinary skills, housekeeping and nursing. Most inspiring to me is my mother's unselfish capacity to give to others, especially her children. She has nurtured us for a lifetime. And this love has allowed us to produce judges, business owners, attorneys, educators – five living generations of professional adults, and children, who are healthy, productive citizens.

We know God, we love, we laugh, we dance, we cook, we clean, we serve, we learn, we teach, we travel, we live a full life, and it started with our "Rock of Ages," Willie Mae Brown.

Biography: *Persis Grayson*
Asbury Center of Baysmont
Kingsport

Twenty years ago, visitors to Persis Grayson's house would likely find her weaving or spinning away at one of her antique spindles. Or she might be sharing her vast knowledge of these age-old arts with one of her many students, teaching them about wool, cotton, flax and other fibers, or showing them how to make their own spinning wheels from spare household items. And, although her health has kept her from being as active as she once was, she now calls Asbury Center at Baysmont home. Persis's reputation as an internationally renowned artisan is still recognized and applauded in the crafting world.

Persis was recently presented with a lifetime achievement award by the Southern Highland Craft Guild for her contributions to the field of crafting as not only an artist but also a teacher and mentor. For more than four decades Persis has fought to keep some of America's most primitive art forms alive by teaching, promoting the public's interest in fiber through hundreds of classes and workshops, and demonstrating spinning, weaving and other crafts at schools, museums and meetings across the country.

In 1971 Persis became the first president of the newly created Handweavers Guild of America, and shortly thereafter helped start the Overmountain Weavers Guild, along with several other dedicated ladies from Kingsport. Persis served on the board of directors and was also a contributing columnist for many years.

In addition to her involvement with the Overmountain Weavers Guild, Persis has long been associated with the Southern Highland Craft Guild, which promotes the various crafts popular in the southern mountains, and holds workshops, fairs and festivals to showcase the talent of its members. She served as president twice, was a member of the board of directors for several years, and is still invited to attend meetings as an honorary member.

Throughout her career, Persis has been actively involved in beginning and promoting several craft schools in the Southeast. She has also served on the board of directors of many of these schools, such as the Penland School of Art in North Carolina, the Arrowmont School in Gatlinburg and the John C. Campbell School.

Although Persis said she enjoys living at Asbury Center at Baysmont, she admits missing the hand woven rugs, bedspreads, curtains, towels and table clothes, placemats, drapes, wall hangings, dresses, shawls and jackets that were so characteristic of her former home.

Regardless, the admiration of her fellow artisans will no doubt be with her for a long time to come.

Biography: *Catherine Ries*
Alexian Brothers Valley Residence
Chattanooga

Catherine is originally from Chicago. She was married and had six children. She also babysat for mothers who could not afford child care. At a very young age she took night classes for 18 months, following which she took physical therapy classes. She was a total of four years in training to be a professional masseuse, or massage therapist as they are commonly called today. She stayed home with her children until they were all in school, then she went to Norwegian American Hospital as an intern, approximately three months after which she got her own clientele. She says she enjoyed working with the public very much and met very interesting people of all kinds. She still knows her massage techniques and practices on residents and caregivers on occasion. She is of Polish descent and helped both her parents in Poland in the restaurant business. She has enjoyed her life and loves helping others.

Biography: *Mary Lou McDonough*
Alexian Brothers Valley Residence
Chattanooga

I am lucky to have had lots of opportunities in my lifetime. I am married and have two girls and one boy and a granddaughter named Heather. She is my precious one.

I have had lots of opportunities to work in different places, too. I worked for the United States Courts with a Federal Circuit Court judge for ten years. This is the highest court next to the Supreme Court. I also worked for a lawyer for ten years.

At one time I worked for the motion picture production company that made the film, "The Wilderness Family."

While living in Indianapolis, I worked for an attaché manufacturing company doing a variety of jobs including sales, but probably my favorite job was in construction. I helped in building houses and drew up the second phase of luxury apartments. I found it to be the most challenging job of all, because I was constantly having to estimate all the materials that we used. It was demanding but my favorite because it kept me on my toes.

Biography: *Pearl Huntley*
Sherry S. Haney, R.N.
Adams Place Assisted Living
Murfreesboro

For several years I was a home health nurse in Lawrenceburg, Tennessee. One of my patients was a maiden lady in her late seventies. Her name was Pearl Huntley. Pearl had only a third grade education formally, but she had been well educated in the game of life. She was full of fun, always had a joke to tell, could play a guitar or a banjo like a pro, and was self-taught. She had been a farmer, and the land she farmed she said she bought with money she won in a poetry contest. As her health further declined and as we became closer, Pearl began to share her poetry with me. She finally gave me a whole stack of poems that she said she had written over the years, and she had no one to leave them to, as she had never married. Each one is signed and dated. Her dream was that some day I might get someone to publish some of her poetry. They are delightful, and paint a touching, and sometimes hilarious, picture of Southern farm life in the 1900s.

ROCK OF AGES

Biography: *Ruth Hurt*
Integrated Health Services of Nashville
Nashville

Back in 1937 when my brother was four months old, we'd have a family gathering and would usually go on picnics. All the Hurt family would pack a picnic. We'd put the kids in little red wagons and take them to the park. Back then when I was growing up, we were poor but we didn't know it. We walked everywhere we went. We still had fun and everybody got along and we loved each other. I've seen a lot of water under the bridge at my age. Yeah, I'm 79 and have seen a lot. There were eight children (actually ten, but two passed on) and Mom and Dad.

Why, I remember when a loaf of bread was a nickel, and if you wanted it sliced it cost 7 cents. We could buy a 24-lb. bag of flour for fifty cents, coffee was a nickel a pound, lard a dime a pound. They didn't have fancy wrapping back then.

In 1935 before my sister was born, we got a washing machine. People back then didn't have mixers and all that stuff. When we'd iron, we'd set the flat iron on a wood-burning cook stove, get the iron hot, then iron. Mom boiled clothes in a big iron pot and washed them on a washboard. She made her own lye soap in place of washing powder. Now that was before we got our washing machine in 1935. On Christmas we got some stuff in a box.

I was born in 1920. I was the oldest child of ten children. My birthday is July 10th. I never married. I stayed home and helped my mom.

I went to Lipscomb School, 1st through 6th grades, then to Howard School starting in the 7th. I quit school after the 11th grade and worked at H.G. Hills grocery from 1945 to 1950. They started me out at $14.00 a week.

When all the children were grown and gone, one of my sisters and I continued to stay home with Mom and Dad. Daddy worked for the City of Nashville for 25 years. He was a smart man; he and Mom raised eight children on $19.20 a week. We were raised in a Methodist church.

My sister and I took care of Mom and Dad when their health was failing. Mama died and we took care of Dad as long as we could. Then in 1984 he was admitted to this home and died in 1988.

Now I'm 79 years old, living in the same nursing home Dad was in. My family visits. I go to exercise class (if I want to). I enjoy looking at magazines, especially *Reminisce*. I get that magazine through the mail every month. Now if you're ever out and about, stop by and see me, but remember my brother Buddy visits every Wednesday afternoon and Lisa from the Activities Department always brings me two bags of popcorn. Buddy and I sit and talk and eat popcorn and drink a cold drink.

Biography: *Nancy B. Britton*
Asbury Center at Baysmont
Kingsport

"Are you Uncle Chuck's mom?" was the question that got me to thinking generationally. It took me at least a second to think who Uncle Chuck was. The third of my tall handsome sons was the father of the bride at this wedding reception where I was the grandmother of the bride. Yes, I was his mother.

Over 30 years ago, this son had married Rose Patryce Guthrie, the youngest child of a large Spartanburg, South Carolina, family. My husband Britt and I enjoyed getting to know not only the parents of our new daughter-in-law but also many more members of the family.

Her sister Nita Rogers had five sons and then adopted a little girl. I had just been talking to two of the sons, Paul and David.

My husband and I had attended the 50th wedding anniversary of the boys' grandparents, held in the Rogers' home in Greer, South Carolina.

When our granddaughter Pat was born, she had about 25 first cousins on her mother's side but none on her father's side until his sister had a baby eleven years ago.

All this is just to suggest to you that my memory holds these many people over the years from their infancy or childhood, their growing up to young and even older adulthood. And their parents have grown older, too.

Then I can look back and remember that once I was the youngest child in a large family until my little brother was born and think of all the things that have happened.

This is one of the delights of growing old, to recall what has gone on and to anticipate the future.

After thinking this way a bit, I saw a little boy comfortably lolling in his stroller and thought for a moment I could almost see him as an old man being pushed in his wheelchair eighty or ninety years from now.

Thinking about it a little more, I thought this is really a very, very small illustration of God's eye view of the world.

ROCK OF AGES

CHAPTER III

OUR LIVES

Part of the mission of Rock of Ages is to give a voice to our seniors residing in senior living facilities and to show the paramount importance of affordable, quality residential care. In this chapter some of Tennessee's older adults share their experiences.

ROCK OF AGES

Assisted Living
Alma Rule
Victorian Square
Rockwood

  We are doing just that, living, at Victorian Square in Rockwood, Tennessee – with a little assistance when needed from a great staff of nurses and aides who truly love and care for us. When we can no longer live alone, how blessed we are to have the many assisted homes from which to choose – homes where we make many new friends with whom we can laugh and still enjoy life together. We, too, get to read, sew, walk, stroll through the flower garden, and many things we had hoped to do after retirement. These facilities also give us a chance to be a blessing instead of a burden to our children. They need and deserve the chance to be building sweet memories with their families just as we did when we were younger.

  Our activities director plans each day with many enjoyable things to do. Sometimes we go down memory lane and share many of life's stories with one another. How interesting they are – people from all walks of life who have traveled the world over, some speaking many different languages. This age group has seen many changes; so much history has been made and dreams have become a reality. We have lived from the day of the Great Depression to the time of space travel and landing on the moon. We are still young in our hearts and excited about the future. Our very versatile director leads us in participating in games, art, music, and one area I have become very interested in, quilting. Several of us ladies have decided to make a quilt, which we plan to sell.

  Sitting quietly in my room one day and thinking about our quilt, a certain poetic name for the quilt came to mind. Being a nine-diamond pattern made with squares, I decided to called it "Victorian Square."

Victorian Square
Alma Rule
Victorian Square
Rockwood

This quilt, named in honor
Of our wonderful home
Has been finished.
It took hours of work
And much time of our own
But our spirits were not diminished.
Each time we met we had laughter and fun
Making the quilt was a joy for everyone.
We chose a pattern that has been used for generations
And went right to work with great determination.
With tired bodies
And hands that tremble
Our needles did not miss a stitch
Or stick a finger

Because we knew how
And wisely used a thimble.
The stitches may not
All be done evenly
But you can rest assured
Each seam done lovingly and carefully
Is made very secure.
Now the thing that makes this quilt
So beautiful and desired
Is the fact that the residents and staff alike have shared
Fabric, thread, thoughtful ideas
And everything needed to become a part
In making each square a piece of art.
To the new owner, whoever you are,
Remember us within your heart
And our gratitude in return
Will be of the greatest measure.
We hope you can display your quilt
With joy and pride
And in doing so, others will become aware
You have a great treasure
Your Victorian Square.

Oh, What A Nice Place This Is
A Tribute to Christian Towers of Gallatin

Dorothy Brown
Christian Towers and The Manor of Gallatin
Gallatin

Our apartments are small, I will agree, but if you don't have too many guests at one time you can manage just fine. There's no worrying about mowing the lawn or scooping the snow, replacing the hot water heater or trimming with paint.

OH, WHAT A NICE PLACE THIS IS!

We have the social room for meetings, playing cards, listening to Bernard play the organ, or just socializing.

OH, WHAT A NICE PLACE THIS IS!

We can sit out back for a breath of fresh air, watch the birds playing in the bird bath, or we can sit out front and watch the children play in the daycare across the street, or we can just sit and watch the world go by.

OH, WHAT A NICE PLACE THIS IS!

We have the van to take us to doctor's appointments or Walmart or the

ROCK OF AGES

grocery store, to Rivergate or Bowling Green shopping malls, and yes, to lunch with our Wednesday Lunch Bunch.

 OH, WHAT A NICE PLACE THIS IS!

We can walk across the street to the Senior Citizens' Center for lunch five days a week, or enjoy a snack and cola from our machines when we don't know what on earth we want to eat.

 OH, WHAT A NICE PLACE THIS IS!

Our apartments are inspected and our incomes investigated, but

 OH, WHAT A NICE PLACE THIS IS!

We have bingo on Tuesday nights and devotions on Thursday nights, and potlucks and birthday parties put on by the most wonderful volunteer ladies.

 OH, WHAT A NICE PLACE THIS IS!

There isn't a building in town that is prettier than ours; with a candle in each window and our star on the roof.

 OH, WHAT A NICE PLACE THIS IS!

Of course, I love my family without reservation, but our wonderful group of people on our board of directors, our staff, our special friends and neighbors are the very best.

 OH, WHAT A NICE PLACE THIS IS!!!!!!

Assisted Living
Harold Russell
Victorian Square
Rockwood

 What better subject to write about than assisted living? For years I have been hearing about the evils of old peoples' homes, and I was pleasantly surprised when I became a resident at Victorian Square. The people here are very nice, and it sure isn't a warehouse of people waiting to die. All the people here for the most part are elderly and they have many interests in life. Some have family in to visit them regularly, others get a kick out of seeing their friends. All in all, they look out for each other. If a resident does not show up on time, it is reported, and someone is sent to look for them. It is almost impossible to misplace something because we soon get used to what we all have; if someone misplaces a can or eyeglasses, someone will soon spot the item and return it to the owner. All these people seem to love to party and have fun. We have all sorts of parties, birthdays, going away and newcomers parties, and baby showers for the younger workers that take care of us. Talking about taking care of us, the attendants keep us clean, do our wash, and serve us great meals. They do minor repair jobs to our things. They are always pleasant and have a happy "Hello" for all of us.

If one of us comes up unhappy, they make a great effort to get us out of the dumps and put a smile on our face. Assisted living has sure changed my mind about being stuck away in a warehouse and waiting for the black angel of death!!!

The Joy of Retirement
Juanita Vaughan
Park Place Retirement Community
Hendersonville

At last! Open spaces in my mind,
Lonely hours to mount the elusive butterfly,
Trailing cobwebs laced with golden harp chords
Strummed in heavenly places.

Or to grasp the tail of the raging tiger
And whip air currents of forgotten follies
Into a froth of youth remembered.

So, if in dotty old age you see me,
Mouth slacked in ancient stupor,
Tread softly, friend, you know not
If you awaken butterfly or raging tiger.

ROCK OF AGES

CHAPTER IV

OUR LESSONS

The seniors in TNAHSA facilities have thousands of years of experience among them to share with later generations. These lessons in life are always gained through a combination of pain and hard work and serve as a guiding light for us today and those yet to be born.

ROCK OF AGES

How Old Are You?

Mary West
Alexian Brothers Community Services
Chattanooga

"You are as old as you feel!" This is a popular statement, but most people live by the "only as old as you look" custom. Our culture seems to have an aversion to the aging process. They use cosmetics, sweet smelling cologne, face-lifts, breast augmentations, and liposuction in order to look young.

Older people have had years of experience and have developed a wealth of knowledge that only age can develop. I attend a day care center that serves disabled individuals who range in age from their fifties to their nineties. Our experiences are innumerable. One man likes to share his WWII experiences with anyone who has the patience to listen. A lady shares the beauty of handwork. She knows how to make lace, a skill that's hardly seen any more because seemingly "nobody" knows how to make it, not even foreigners whose goods are exported and sold in our stores. We have capable, retired ministers, mothers, fathers, computer experts – you name it. I can only expend my own experiences.

I started my work career as a soda jerk. Then I took a tour in the Air Force where I was able to work side by side with the early astronauts in learning the techniques of instrument flying as well as maintaining flight simulators and, later, jet simulators. I like to remember and brag that I worked with Colonel Chuck Yeager, now a general.

After the Air Force, I attended college and received a degree in Biblical Education. That qualified me for working on the foreign mission field of Brazil, a land of contrasts of good and evil. One of the first things I saw was a dead black chicken with a bottle of wine placed in the middle of the road as an offering to Satan. We later met Christians who were loyal to God, and we shared the Lord with them. I mean "shared" because we learned from each other. Many tried to mix Macumba, or witchcraft, with Christianity. That did not work. I traveled extensively and met a lot of people of different ages who were very skilled and knowledgeable.

My last work career was as a social worker and counselor. I really learned there.

As we gain knowledge, our bodies continue to age. We have to depend on others for things we used to do easily. We would like to be identified by what we can do, not by what we can't do. As disabled individuals, we each have to cope with losses of strong, able bodies, ability to walk, drive anywhere we want to go, ability to see, speak, work like we used to, and the hardest of all losses – control of your own life.

A friend, knowing how hard I took it having to retire, sent me an appropriate card. On the front was a smug looking cat and bright letters with the message:

> Ah, birthdays, a time to rejoice in the coming of
> wisdom, the maturing of senses and the passage
> of time. Truly, getting older is a privilege and a
> time when people begin to treat you with respect.

I opened the card and the sound of uncontrollable laughter came out. The cat was doubled over with laughter. This gave me an opportunity to laugh at a serious social problem: discrimination toward the elderly.

You will one day age, as it is something nobody can escape. You'll find it in red eyes, white hair, tooth and gum problems, etc. Remember that and treat the aged the way you would like to be treated.

The Bible tells us "For God so loved the world that He gave His only begotten Son, that whoever believes in Him, should not perish but have everlasting life." (John 3:16 NKJV)

How old am I? I consider myself ageless since I'm going to live forever. How do you count your age? As looks, feelings, years, or experience? Ageless sounds good to me!

I Led Three Lives
Austin Flint Hubbard
Alexian Village of Tennessee
Signal Mountain

For me, life has been in three parts. Shakespeare saw a person's life as having seven ages in the lines of his play *As You Like It*. But for me, life has three parts. I have already lived through the first and second; now I am in the third and last part.

My life began when I was about three years old, and I found myself living with my parents and siblings in a big house. That house and grounds were my world. Later my sphere expanded to the town where we lived. It was an unfamiliar world to begin with. But it was a given world, one I accepted the way it was, something I myself had little or no control of. Sometimes I thought my family was wonderful and I was filled with love; at other times I wished they were different. Nevertheless, they were what they were.

I was continually filled with curiosity about what all this stuff around me was. What was it? What made it do what it did? It wasn't that I could change things; that never occurred to me. Things were the way they were. But I was curious about the whys and wherefores. From time to time something happened that changed things, like a new baby brother or a collie dog coming into my life. These things were exciting and I immediately related to them in my own way. One thing always concerned me: was I smart enough, good enough, able to hold my own?

Sometimes things were bad: I did wrong and I knew it, or I felt sick, or something scary happened like the time I was in the family car and it rolled over. But when a frightening thing happened, you went along with it as best you could. If it was your fault, you felt sorry and you tried to forget it. If it wasn't your fault, you wondered why it happened, but you accepted it anyway. In short, in the first part of my life, everything was given. My job was to adjust to it, play my role correctly, and learn about this world I had been made a part of.

The big change for me into part two of my life was when I realized that it was going to be my responsibility to do something myself: not to just take from this life I had been given, but to contribute to it. My parents, in effect, wished me well, but they and my siblings had their own jobs to do, and now I was ready to do mine. I looked around for opportunities, trained in schools and tried to develop skills. I went off to war.

Part two of my life meant goodbye to my old family. But I acquired a new family: marriage, children, and the greater family of my associates on my job and in my community. Instead of depending on my parents for leadership, I needed to provide leadership myself. My mistakes were my own fault, and there was no one else to blame them on. I felt the responsibility to contribute to this sphere I was now a part of.

The difference for me now was that life was not entirely a given. To some extent at least, I felt the responsibility of creating life myself, and also helping others on the road with me. I was not just a conformer, or a learner anymore: I was meant to be a doer and a contributor to life. I still made mistakes and felt sorry for them; people still did things to me. Sometimes I was hurt by the necessity of living in this world. But all in all, as I acquired the responsibility for other people, I felt I was beginning to know what life is all about. No longer was everything a mystery: it now began to make sense, albeit still puzzling at times.

Most of the old family, the ones I had begun with, were still here, but now they were on the same footing as I. We were friends now, on a different level, in phase two of my life. In some ways, we were closer than we'd been before.

The change from the second into the third stage of my life, the one I'm in now, was not as well marked. There was no graduation ceremony from two into three, more a gradual moving. As the old family went on ahead of me, I acquired new families from time to time, and my job was more advisory than direct manipulation.

It was sort of like building a house. In stage one you see people's houses, you wonder about them, you get ideas about them, and you learn to build. In stage two you know how to build, you build a house yourself and occupy it. In stage three you move to helping other people, advising others if you will, in building their houses.

Each stage, I found, has its pluses and minuses. The first stage was exciting in learning new things, but could be dangerous as you made mistakes or had misunderstandings. On the other hand, you had your parents to help you, correct you, make it all right. In the second stage you moved into unexplored territory, but your mistakes were more serious and hurt more perhaps. Things weren't completely laid out for you: you had a chance to lay out your own life, for better or for worse. In the third stage, you feel the lack of building things yourself, changing your environment for the better, but there is the glory in participating with the joys and sorrows of others.

They say the difference between human beings and animals is that we have a memory to learn from our mistakes. Of course, many animals do this too, but not to the extent that is prevalent with humans. Perhaps it's better not to remember too much. On the other hand, I don't want to lose the understanding for which I've strived so many years. For better or worse, however, here I am in stage three of this life in which I find myself. Now, even this third role in the drama of life is coming to a close. What will the review of the play be when I go up yonder? We shall see!

OUR LESSONS

Health Care From Heaven
James Wendell Wooten
Wesley Highland Towers
Memphis, TN

There is so much about TennCare, and other health care plans. It's an old truism and to some extent still a true truism, that you don't have anything if you don't have your health. Most of out interest focuses on physical and mental health, but as Christian people, we should be interested in spiritual health as well.

For those who are disciples of the Hebrew prophet Jesus of Nazareth, let us think about health care from heaven through Christ.

Luke tells a story (Luke 5:17-32) about a time when Jesus was teaching and a paralyzed man was lowered through a hole in the roof of the house where Jesus was, so that the man might be healed. First, Jesus proclaims to the man that his sins are forgiven. Then, after the Pharisees and Scribes protest, Jesus commands the man to get up off his bed and go home; the man promptly did, causing quite a stir among everyone there. After this, Jesus left the house and found a man named Levi, who we know as Matthew, in his tax collecting office. Jesus asked Levi to follow him and they went to Levi's home for a big party, attended mostly by other tax collectors. Again the Pharisees and Scribes protested, and in Jesus' reply we are given some of the best news ever to be told: "Those who are well have no need of a physician, but those who are sick, I have not come to call the righteous, but the sinners to repentance." (Luke 5:31-32)

Good doctors are also willing to risk their own lives in order to help their patients. Thirty-one years ago, Dr. Jonas Salk invented the polio vaccine and used himself as a guinea pig for research. Several years ago, he began to try to find a vaccine for the AIDS virus, and again he used himself as a test case. Many doctors and nurses have lost their lives in the pursuit of healing.

In the case of Jesus the physician, the same is true. In order to bring the healing message of God's love...to tax collectors...and murderers...and prostitutes...and social outcasts...and racists, Jesus risked rejection and ridicule...perhaps even death.

In fact, because of all that he did in a sick, sinful world, Jesus lost his life.

Let's Have a Party
Ena Eble Peavyhouse
Victorian Square
Rockwood

I would like to share with all of you my reasons why each and every one of us should be registered and voting in all elections. It seems all too many aren't registered, and those who are don't bother to vote except in presidential elections, if then.

It is important to familiarize ourselves with local and state problems as well as federal. This would enable us to make better choices in both presidential and state elections. The representatives we send to Washington need to know our views on how we feel they should vote on bills that will help us as senior citizens. They cannot represent us properly if we do not let them know. They do take heed if a registered voter tells them which bills we feel should be passed and sent to the President for his signature. If we do not agree with a bill, we should urge the President to veto that bill and suggest amendments for Congress to consider so the bill can become law.

Too many people, especially senior citizens, say, "Oh, I don't bother to vote. One vote won't make any difference." To those, I want to tell you how important ONE single vote has been in the past. I will list the ones I feel are so very important.

    1776: One vote gave America English language instead of German.
    1845: One vote brought Texas into the Union.
    1868: One vote saved President Andrew Johnson from impeachment.
    1876: One vote gave Rutherford B. Hayes the presidency.
    1923: One vote gave Adolph Hitler leadership of the Nazi Party.

I ask you to think about this last one. If only one person who didn't bother to vote had voted against Hitler's being the leader of the Nazi Party, how many lives might have been spared? History would have been changed for all of us, not just the ones who served in the military and were killed or wounded, but families all over the world. If Hitler had failed then, perhaps he would not have, with the help of Italy and Japan, terrorized the entire world and killed and maimed untold millions. In the United States alone, 1,000 veterans of World War II are still dying each day.

Another example of how history can be changed when so few bother to vote is when the USSR (now Russia) became a communist country. Only 5% of USSR's citizens were actually members of the Communist Party, but the few were able to control millions for many years.

Perhaps you are wondering why I chose "Let's Have a Party" as the title of this writing. In the 1960s I was very involved in one of the major political parties. I was appointed to the State Committee (California) and ran for Los Angeles County Committee and won. I was a "Golden Girl Hostess" at our convention in 1960. While I was "Toast Mistress," in one of my speeches I used the title "Let's Have a Party." I ended that speech by saying: "Join a political party...perhaps some of you will join me in my party."

By being so involved in my party, I came to the realization that I was in the wrong party. In early 1970, I changed my registration and haven't missed an election since. When I moved to Victorian Square Assisted Living, one of the first things I did was update my address with the Election Commission.

I urge you to join a political party, even if it isn't my party. If we don't register and vote, do we really have the right to complain when others decide our lives for us?

All About Jesus
    Lucille Skaggs
    Wesley on the Ridge
    Jonesboro, AR

I was walking down a road one day; it was the straight and narrow road I had been on for a while.

Suddenly I saw a man walking along with me. He said, "Where are you

OUR LESSONS

going?" and I said, "I'm going to Heaven, what about you?"

He said, "I've already been there with our Father for a long time. I've seen the heavy load you have been carrying and how hard it's been. I know all your heartaches and I have seen all your tears. I know every burden that you are carrying up that hill.

"I've known you for a long time, and I would have helped you carry that load if only you had let me. When you walk through that lonesome valley, I'll go with you too. You see, all those people that hanged me on a tree, I prayed that God would forgive them for they know not what they do. You see, I'm your Savior and I want to bear your burdens because I love you, my Daughter. I'm that same Jesus that they hanged on the tree to take away your sins. They didn't take my life, I gave it freely for you, my dear Friend."

Synonyms

M.C. Morriss Keller
Wesley Highland Towers
Memphis

I am not an embryo from my mother's womb;
I am a soul created with love and wisdom.
I am an artist, mother, and grandmother.

My earthly spirit descended from the throne of England and persons of character in America, including Patrick Henry. He believed in "liberty or death" for the freedom of Spiritual Right.

As a child I was taught that I did not belong to myself. The world did not belong to me. I was here to think of others by whatever means I had. Because "I had," I was to give of myself and count for something beyond the "self."

I have anguished through the wars, beginning with World War II, Korea, Vietnam, and on. They tore my beautiful world apart. I, too, had to learn and grow some more.

I put aside my dreams of teaching fine arts. I was a professional businessperson for thirty years, with my own firm.

During the years I was the provider for my loving family, I drew upon the resources of my childhood. I was always seeing the "withinness echo" of my assigned responsibility when the opportunity presented itself.

I met many wonderful persons along my journey. Each had their own uniqueness and capabilities, whether large or small. I learned to respect differences.

Within the reflections of my sameness I am still the earthly source of myself. I am my own synonym.

In my visions I see the TRUTHS of learning and giving. TRUTHS live forever. Each person blessed by being on the earthly journey has an eternal future through the greatest gate of all:

"REAL LOVE"
Grow future, grow with "love for all."
You can do it.
GROW!

ROCK OF AGES

In Quietness

Florence Irwin
Sycamores Terrace Retirement Community
Nashville

Mankind has always had a need for some quietness in life. Since we live in a climate of tension, in a noisy, confused, turbulent world, we have a great need to develop a sense of quietness and calm. The Bible teaches us a way of being quiet and alone with God. From the book of Isaiah one reads, "In quietness and confidence shall be your strength." From the Psalmist we find, "Be still and know I am God," and again, "He leadeth me beside still waters, He restoreth my soul." Elijah the Prophet, after being in battle, exhausted, depressed, and fearing for his life, hid in a cave and was told by angels to come out and go to the top of the mountain to hear God's voice who would give him a message. Elijah went. While listening for God's voice, a great storm came, an earthquake, and a terrible fire, but in all of this there came a great calm. Out of the calm and quietness came the voice of the spirit of God. "The still small voice."

The impact of Paul's conversion was so great, instead of staying in Damascus or going back to Jerusalem, he felt the need for a period of meditation and prayer. So he went to the desert to commune with God in solitude. Even Christ sought out quiet places. Just after His baptism in the Jordan River, He went to be alone in the wilderness for forty days to prepare Himself for His ministry, which was to come. At another time, after speaking to a crowd of 5,000 and feeding them, He left to find a quiet place of peace and rest. In the Garden of Gethsemane He prayed alone while the disciples slept.

It was Emerson who said, "I like the quiet church before the service begins." Perhaps it prepared him to be more receptive to what was to come in this service. A pastor of a large church kept a record of hymns used during a ministry of 30 years; high among the favorites was "Dear Lord and Father of mankind." One of the verses reads:

> Drop they still dues of quietness
> Till all our striving cease
> False from our souls the strain and stress
> The beauty of thy peace.

It is a comfort to know that God is ready to nurture and renew our spirit – alone with Him, one can find strength for the day and confidence for the future. As Phillips Brooks looked over the sleeping town of Bethlehem one starry night, he wrote the lyric for the Christmas carol "O Little Town of Bethlehem." Some of the lines are:

> How silently, how silently,
> The wondrous gift is given;
> So God imparts to human hearts,
> The blessings of His heaven.

So God works silently and wondrously. We know of many persons who have achieved greatness in spite of handicaps, but not before time spent alone with

OUR LESSONS

God. Handel's biographer said of him, "His health and his fortune had reached its lowest ebb. He became blind, his right side paralyzed and his money was all gone. His creditors seized him and threatened to imprison him. For a brief time he was tempted to give up the fight, but in the quietness of his studio, alone with his blindness and with God, he rebounded again to compose the Messiah."

I am reminded of our own Tennessee poet Jane Merchant who, in spite of her debilitating disease, in the quietness of her room, most surely received strength and inspiration from God to become a writer. Going back to her childhood, she wrote the little poem, "Growing Days," which reflects her thoughts on quietness. It reads:

> You've had as much excitement as you should
> Our mother very often used to say
> The fun you've had won't do you any good
> Till it has settled down in to stay
> So listen to the creek and nibble cress
> Go count the grass and catch up with your living
> So we would revel in green idleness
> And never realize what she was giving.

Some may have a special place or time for quietness. It may be in the quietness of home, walking along, doing some task, outdoors with nature or an early morning devotion reading the Bible.

In one of the upper rooms I read of a lady who grew up on a small farm in the Appalachian Mountains. She found a special place – a hill, which she called "my mountain." She liked to walk to the top, lie on the slope, and meditate on the meaning of life. It gave her a feeling of being close to God and became a holy place where she could meet Him and find strength for living. Think for a moment and see how many blessings have come to us silently. One writer made a list. She wrote: "Silently, the new green leaves grow. Silently, the earth moves around the sun, turns on its axis, brings day and night; it tilts so changing the seasons. Silently, a baby grows to adulthood (vocal chords not withstanding)."

Those who must live in the silent world of deafness could tell us of the blessings of the silent written word. One needs to remember the need to be alone; not only in bad times but in good times; one should have quiet time to be grateful and meditate on the goodness that has come to us. Mark said in his gospel "6:31": "Come away by yourselves, and rest awhile."

In our place or time of quietness do we listen to God's voice? A Peanuts comic strip cartoon shows Lucy standing, looking up at the rain. She says the familiar lines: "Rain, rain, go away! Come again some other day!" It keeps on raining, so Lucy looks toward heaven and declares, "Are you listening?"

Just like Lucy, we often want God to listen and assure us, but do we stop to listen to Him? God speaks to us in different ways: through the Bible, through people, and through the beauty of God's creation, but most of all through the Holy Spirit, the still small voice within our hearts.

In order to develop a sense of quietness and calm, by which we might renew our spirit and gain strength for living, let us find a quiet place, be still, listen, and know He is God.

ROCK OF AGES

CHAPTER V

OUR WORDS

Rock of Ages was also conceived to showcase the abilities and talents of today's vibrant older adults. Far from helpless and dependent, the works below show that Tennessee's senior citizens are quick of mind, sharp of tongue, deep of thought and full of wit.

ROCK OF AGES

Twilight
>*Ruby McDill*
>Belmont Village
>Nashville

Twilight shadows bring the close of day
And the setting of the sun in the west
Is like a great, disappearing ball of fire,
Which, after a day of work, has gone to rest.
Trees stir gently in the twilight breeze
Where nests of birds are still and quiet.
The moon is seen faintly through the trees
And over the world drops
The curtain of night.

Siblings
>*Sherry S. Haney, R.N.*
>Adams Place Assisted Living
>Murfreesboro

Once they ran lightheartedly
Through meadow and forest glen
Now they carefully push their walkers –
How they'd love to run again.

Once they drove T-models
And rushed off to play croquet
Now they sit sedately in their apartments
And nap for half the day.

Once they loved to party
And could stay up half the night
Now they need help with a bath
And to get their clothes on right.

Now Sister waits for Brother
To come creeping down the hall
And when they spy each other
Their big smiles tell it all.

Ode to a Tree

Rose Love Tate
Wesley Highland Manor
Memphis

You once stood tall and stately
Leafy branches reached the sky,
You gave us shelter from the sun,
To everyone passing by.

But time has passed – you too have aged
Your leaves no longer green.
Your limbs have truly gone with the wind,
Or they start to break and lean.

We sadly watched each minute
As they cut you down,
And many thoughts were with us
As limbs fell to the ground.

Man can replace a building
Exactly as it stood,
Or a house can easily take its place,
It's only brick or wood.

And then a line from a poem
Suddenly came to me,
Men can do so many things,
But only God can make a tree.

Hands

Rubye Longley Hundley
McKendree Village
Hermitage

I looked at my hands to see
Mama's hands as they used to be,
aging and never quite still–
some other task to fulfill.
Hands that soothed a fevered brow,
stilled a crying child somehow.
Hands that caressed a sleepy head
restless in her bed.
Hands that could sew and bake,
make a birthday cake!
Hands that scattered seed,
for the birds to feed.

ROCK OF AGES

Hands careworn, but gentle in touch,
during my childhood did so much.
Then one day, with a tear and a sigh,
she waved to me, her last good-bye!

In the Mining Museum
Mardelle S. Bourdon
Uplands Retirement Village
Pleasant Hill

They've stood so long before my searching heart,
These silent, haunted men with tired faces,
So young, so silent, so resigned,
Yet, shouting of despair and of this place.
Within the mural, I find again,
The age-old struggle for bread and butter.
The gray and loveless walls
Speak obscenities as vile
As bayonets and guns of metal.
Rusting axe and broken shovel confirm
The torture of their lives.

Single child in the midst, not yet ten years old,
Denied the skinny-dip of boyish laughter,
By Labor's crimes untold.
Just too tired from heaving his load
To see the beach's silky sand.
Never allowed to lie on his back
To peer at a far-away land,
Nor talk to the moon-faced clouds,
Who smiled and winked at him.
No time for winking at them.

A pale man has but one boot.
Is the other still colliered below?
Did he miss it when he trudged on?
Did anyone want to know?
Did he live alone in the shack by the slag,
Where the gray, greasy rainwater ran?
Are his shirts all in tatters and no one cared, or
Was that all that he had?

They came to find Life and stand so betrayed.
What robbed them of sunshine and summer,
While Life shines so brightly for me?
Green grass grows tall round the miners' incline, and
The miners just stare from their grimy, black wall.
They couldn't have seen it, at all.

To Wait for a Train
Lily Hardy
Morningside of Franklin
Franklin

To wait for a train,
always gave him pain
he tried to cross first,
to his sorrow
but the train was too fast,
and he didn't get past.
They're holding his
funeral tomorrow

Yellow Butterfly
Charlotte H. Alexander
Asbury Place Retirement Center
Chattanooga

Sitting on the Patio one day,
A yellow Butterfly came my way
You are such a lovely thing
Yellow Butterfly on the wing.

Sipping from one flower to the next
How do you know which flower is best?
Silently you fly away
Come again another day.

Yellow butterfly on the wing,
You are such a lovely thing.

He Was Taking Her Home at Twilight
Lily Hardy
Morningside of Franklin
Franklin

He was taking her home at twilight
The night was cool and still
In the west the sun was setting
On yon distant hill
They were walking quite close together
You would think he would kiss her now
But he was a country boy
and she was a Jersey cow.

ROCK OF AGES

Saturday Morning
>*Sherry S. Haney, R.N.*
>Adams Place Assisted Living
>Murfreesboro

The ash embraces the cedar
Standing sentinel by the creek.
The pleated woodpecker
Gathers breakfast with his beak.

The sun's rays streak across the sky
Painting shades of coral hue,
As we sit and drink our coffee,
Planning other things to do.

The squirrel grinds and chips a nut,
While the flycatcher sings his song.
And the hummers fight over the feeders –
They do it all day long.

As we hear the distant rumblings
Of a thunderstorm to the West,
We stop to count our blessings
For we know this life is best.

Noon-Time
>*Jeanette Mandigo*
>Sycamores Terrace Retirement Community
>Nashville

When the clock on the wall lifts its two hands together to pray,
Then you will know it is noon for that day.

Although, if darkness fills the sky,
'Tis midnight – Oh, my!

Reasons for Love
>*Rose Love Tate*
>Wesley Highland Manor
>Memphis

Some people love, as the saying goes,
For sentimental reasons,
While others have to be inspired

By the usual change in seasons.
Such as in Spring their fancies turn
To thoughts of love and then,
When Summer makes a change to Fall
Well, they're in love again.
Yes, some folks have their reasons,
Perhaps they're great or small
But I love you my dear for...well,
For no good reason at all.

We, The People
Sterling Brownlow
Hewitt House Assisted Living
Pulaski

We, the people of the United Sates,
Live in a land where our forefathers predestined our fates.
They worked out a Constitution for us to be governed by
Headed by a President, The White House to occupy.
They created different laws and regulations
And did this with level headed determination.
We know full well we have an obligation
To live by, and carry out, their legislation.
We are one nation under God, indivisible
To think any other way would be inadvisable.
The Constitution was to establish justice,
Each to be treated equal without prejudice.
We are to have liberty to do as we please
And perform all of our duties with ease.
The Constitution promotes the general welfare,
There's no other country that can compare.
We have been, and still are, one nation under God
So let's give thanks for His land on which we trod.
Let's stand behind our President in his endeavors
And continue to have a good nation forever.

Where are the Fairies?
Mardelle S. Bourdon
Uplands Retirement Community
Pleasant Hill

Where are the fairies that I once knew,
Who lived in the meadow where the blue birds flew?
They welcomed me then, to the shadowy deep.
To their tiny house, 'neath the clover sweep.
"Won't you come in?" was the whispered greeting.
I heard it well and welcomed our meeting.

ROCK OF AGES

"Now, sit right here, I'm brewing some tea.
And you must share your dreams with me."

She was a grandmother fairie, I knew then,
She spun woolen yarns and fed her hens.
They lay jelly-bean eggs, spangled and sweet.
She served them with tea, whenever we'd meet.
Now, I go back to the meadow green,
And sit by the slow, meandering stream.
I search for the clover cottage of yore,
I yearn to tap on the tiny front door.

But, time has taken away the sheen,
From my six-year-old's joy and the fairie queen.
There must be a reason I knew her then,
There must be a time we'll meet again.

Will she be waiting, as my eyes grow dim?
Will she welcome me to Eternity's glen?

The Days Between
Juanita Vaughan
Park Place Retirement Community
Hendersonville

I was quite upset today,
A good friend said to me,
"Of all the jobs there are to do,
A nurse I could not be.
I would be so depressed
Each time my patient died,
To remember all the things I'd done,
How very hard I'd tried."

It never had occurred to me
That I could really heal;
That was not my aim in life
For training in this field.
I'm sure sometimes we push too hard
To try to have our say,
But tying leaves upon the trees
Was never Nature's way.

There's a time to be born, a time to die,
In both we play a part;
But the love we give in the days between
Is the beat of a Nurse's heart.

Numbers

Sherry S. Haney, R.N.
Adams Place Assisted Living
Murfreesboro

I sometimes wonder which one is me
Am I 6105 or 5743?
And to make a call, what do I do?
Do I push 893 or 1872?
And if through the door I wish to go
Is it 1871 or 1870?
And then, to get in my car at night
(At least half the time, I can't get it right)
I simply want to open the door
So what do I push – is it 6204?
Or maybe the number's 2573.
Oh, my gosh, what can it be?

And if my hubby I want to call
I pick up the receiver – can't remember at all!
Is it 2867 or 8495?
Oh, my gracious sakes alive!!!!!!!!!
With him I simply want to talk
Think I'll forget the phone
And just take a walk.
A whole lot quicker the deed would be done.
Oh! Maybe the number is 1751!

And then to the doctor I make a call
Well, I can't get through to him at all.
"If you want this, push number 1,
Or maybe to rapidly get the job done,
You'd be better off to push number 2."
(For sure, no human will talk to you!)

THAT'S IT!!! I'VE HAD IT!!!
I'm going to bed! Lie down on my pillow,
Rest my weary head. I'll just burrow in and hide my face
And relieve my mind of the numbers that race
Over and over, back and forth through my muddled mind
Oh gosh, who's that calling? The phone says 2599.

A Yellow Rose
Frank Willson
Arbor Terrace
Knoxville

A yellow rose bloomed by the side of the road.
That brightened my day and lightened my load.

When evening drew nigh, I used to wander.
to a secluded spot my time to squander.
To commune with nature amid the tall trees,
to relax and make love in the evening breeze.
I'd stop by the road and pick a bouquet,
in order to please her and hear her say, I love you.
I've never known a fragrance more rare,
than the yellow rose I placed in her hair.
Her laughter was music and love was all mine,
the moments we shared were like very rare wine.
She banished my cares and brightened my day,
I live for the moment I can hear her say, I love you.
When alas time changes, things come to a close,
what happened to us only heaven knows.
Now I sit alone among the tall trees,
to a whippoorwill call on the evening breeze.
The yellow rose died and had not one leaf,
as though in sympathy for my grief.
Now I know it's all over and I'll never again hear,
her whisper to me in tones oh so dear,
I love you!

Grandmother to Granddaughter
Rubye Longley Hundley
McKendree Village
Hermitage

Come visit with me little one,
your life has just begun.
Whatever path you take
is the choice you make.
Seek knowledge and truth always,
God's commandments obey.
Keen of mind, pure in heart,
what better way to start?
Be happy in your work and play,
may joy and gladness fill every day.
Be kind in thought, word and deed
helpful in others' need.

May God grant you insight,
To choose a future bright.
You are my ray of sunshine,
little granddaughter of mine!

The Statue of Liberty
Sterling Brownlow
Hewitt House Assisted Living
Pulaski

The Statue of Liberty, in all splendor and ardor,
Just stands there in New York Harbor,
Waiting to welcome strangers from afar
To this beautiful country, no one she will bar.
She stands there as a symbol of liberty and justice for all
Just the thought of it keeps us enthralled.
She has stood there for one hundred years,
Witnessing people coming with eyes filled with tears.
Millions of immigrants have come our way,
Hoping and praying for a better day.
They have come from countries where they were oppressed,
To fulfill hopes and dreams they have possessed.
Many of them failed and went back sadly,
While the majority stayed on and worked gladly.
They worked hard and practiced self-denial,
Through many hard times and many trials.
Many immigrants rose from rags to riches
By working hard, even digging ditches.
We are so glad they like our way of life,
To endure so much hardship and strife.
May the Statue stand long after being rejuvenated.
And may many of our problems be eliminated.
May the U.S. continue to have peace and prosperity,
But not to the extent of austerity.
The 100th anniversary has been celebrated,
We hope the effects have been calibrated
To the extent that its results have been far reaching,
And promotes good will that we are teaching.
May the Statue stand one hundred more years,
And we shall press on without fears.
The beacon of light held in her right hand
Shall forever welcome ships and people to our land.

ROCK OF AGES

One Magic Hour
Vera Maye Ward
Asbury Place
Chattanooga

Is there too great a fee for your caress?
Will it end with heartbreak and with pain?
And all the old familiar nights of loneliness?
I, who loved you all these years, in wonder ask
what can we hope for at last?
One more magic hour when we forget
our dreams may never be.
While your charm and power sweep o'er me like a flame,
and we're consumed by love's fire,
That we again, may never claim.

Love, Joe
Juanita Vaughan
Park Place Retirement Community
Hendersonville

There's a flower there on the window sill,
It's wilted and really should go,
But it's the only one "Our Lady" has had,
So I'll leave it a day or so.
Someone slipped it in one night
With a note – "Love, Joe."
I'm sure I saw that special bud
On a bush the hospital grows.
The vase – sparkling, diamond cut crystal –
I saw it in room number nine;
The flower it held was a pink rose then,
But it's red, for love, this time.

The rose was picked by the angel hand
That wrote the note – "Love, Joe."
To ordinary folks, it makes no sense;
He died many years ago.
Each day, Joe comes to visit –
I can tell when he's here by her smile.
Where true love dwelt, no need for words,
Just sit and dream awhile.

When her cup of life is completely filled
And it comes her time to go.
He'll come and they'll walk hand in hand down the path –
"Our Lady" and her "Love, Joe."

Words
Mary Shires
Sycamores Terrace Retirement Community
Nashville

"A word fitly spoken is like apples of gold in pictures of silver."
(Proverbs 25:11)

I hope that I shall never be
Devoid of curiosity
About the meaning of a word
That I have never seen nor heard.
I hope, when of a word I'm wary,
I'll always seek a dictionary
For help and counsel as a friend;
To give interpretation the desired end.

Bondage
Rose Love Tate
Wesley Highland Manor
Memphis

I thought I had swept my heart's house clean;
Each corner and crevice and shelf;
That there were no signs whatever of you.
I was feeling quite proud of myself.
But in spite of my trying to leave you behind,
You seem to have stayed in my subconscious mind.
So I guess it's no use of my worry and strife.
You continue to be a part of my life.
Yes, I thought I was free as I wanted to be,
That things were going alright.
But no matter what goes, you are there, I suppose
'Cause I dreamed about you last night.

If I Were Skilled
Doris Davis
Cumberland Ridge Assisted Living
Crossville

If I were skilled so that with brush and color I could take the turquoise blue from out the sky: the rose and gold of the sunset and the silver from a star in the sky and place them onto a canvas the picture could not compare to the light that shines in my mother's eyes and the silver that streaks her hair. If I could capture the laughter of the rushing little brook and the serenity of a shady nook and write them into a symphony the sound would never be as sweet as the sound of my mother's voice as she sings a lullaby to me. Someday her face will be near and her voice no longer heard but deep within my memory will remain her songs and her word.

The Prodigal Son
Juanita Vaughan
Park Place Retirement Community
Hendersonville

The patient I had was extremely bad,
Victim of a massive stroke;
His sons and daughters were gathered there,
Not one word the old man spoke.
I could tell the children had a problem,
Whispered softly, looking at Dad,
Then beckoned me step outside the door
And told me the trouble they had.
Seems one of his children was missing,
Had been gone for many a year;
Truly the black sheep of the family,
Addicted to gambling and beer.
He and his Dad had always had trouble,
And one fight led to another;
His leaving had broken their Daddy's heart,
And hastened the death of their Mother.
Still, they thought it right to call him –
After all, it was his Father, too.
They decided it best to warn me,
Didn't know what their Father might do.
For hours it seemed we waited,
The old man nearer to death;
The missing son appeared in the doorway,
Smell of whiskey on his breath.
His hair was long and unruly,
He had yellow broken teeth;
When he bent to kiss his Father,
I saw prison striped clothes underneath.
He took the wasted hand of his Father,
Said, "Dad! You remember your Si."
You would think Heaven's gates had opened
From the look in the old man's eye;
He smiled and I'm sure he forgave him
All of the wrong he had done.
There were tears in the eyes of his brothers and sisters,
As they welcomed the "Prodigal Son."

The Future
> *Rose Love Tate*
> Wesley Highland Manor
> Memphis

It isn't the NOW that I'm minding so much;
I manage to spend every day
In such a mad rush, that I don't have the time
To miss the things you might do or say
But when I grow older, with time on my hands
I'm sure I won't sleep a wink
My time will be spent in useless repent
I'll have time to miss you – and think.

Summer's End
> *Mardelle S. Bourdon*
> Uplands Retirement Community
> Pleasant Hill

Leather skinned now, the Oak leaf,
Mottled in summer's Heat
Rests in Jade Pine bows
Quiet, waiting, discreet.

In scorching sand, hurrying beetles
Clutch grassy, dry wisps
Of filmy, gray mantle,
Near twigs, charred and crisp.

Before our eyes, waters glide
On oil-skinned surface, red,
Releasing a heron of knobby knees,
With a crown upon his head.
Scraggly feathers lift him high,
Claiming relief from the sun,
Leathery leaf, arched and dry,
Seems glad that Summer is done.

ROCK OF AGES

CHAPTER VI

OUR FAITH

Through all of these works, a common thread is the importance of faith. Whether expressed through wonder at creation, the gift of love or faith in a design greater than ourselves, Tennessee's older adults have used their faith as a foundation to achieve peace in this life.

ROCK OF AGES

He is Here!

Mary L. Chapman
Alexian Brothers Community Services
Chattanooga

"He is not here,"
Said the innkeeper to the shepherds with a weary sigh.
"Oh, but He must be, for we have heard the angels from on high,
Tell about the Babe who is to be our king.
Just this very night we heard them sing,
'For unto you is born a Savior this glorious day,
And in Bethlehem, wrapped in swaddling clothes, He doth lay!'
The innkeeper then said, "There was a child born this night in yon stable,
To some Nazarenes here for the taxing, but it doesn't fit your fable."
The shepherds found the Baby in the manger and joyfully exclaimed:
"He is here!"

"He is not here,"
Said King Herod to the wisemen who had traveled far.
"Oh, but He must be for we have been following this star,
Which is a fulfillment of the prophecy of a great king.
Our gifts of gold, frankincense and myrrh to Him we bring."
Herod's counselors searched all the prophecies that were around,
And they declared Bethlehem was the place He would be found.
The Magi followed the star until it stood still,
There they found the child of peace and goodwill.
They worshipped Him with exceeding great joy, saying;
"He is here!"

"He is not here,"
Said the kinfolk as Mary and Joseph searched among the crowd,
For their twelve-year-old son of whom they were so very proud.
"Oh, but he must be – we have traveled all day,
Surely He hasn't been lost along the way.
Let us return to the temple in Jerusalem fair."
Siting amid the doctors and lawyers they found Him there.
Mary asked, "Why have you been such a worry and bother?"
He replied, "Don't you know I must be about the business of my Father?"
Mary and Joseph looked upon the child with amazement and said;
"He is here."

"He was not here,"
Said Martha sorrowfully, "Or else Lazarus would not have died.
We sent Him word – He could have been here if He had tried."
Jesus was a close friend of Lazarus, Martha and Mary,
They all wondered why so long He would tarry.
As Jesus came to the gravesite and joined in the weeping,
He said, "Be comforted; he is not dead, only sleeping."
He called and Lazarus from the grave arose!

OUR FAITH

Martha and Mary rushed to unwrap the grave clothes.
They glorified God as they lovingly proclaimed:
"He is here!"

"He is not here,"
Said the two sadly as they walked to Emmaus.
"We thought He was Messiah sent to deliver us,
But He was delivered to the Romans by our own Sanhedrin Court.
Crucified, buried, now His body is gone – risen by Mary's report."
They were joined by a stranger as they walked,
And they listened with a burning heart as He talked.
They asked Him to sup with them, to hear more of what He said,
Then their eyes were opened as He blessed and broke the bread.
With gladdened hearts and joyful acclamation they proclaimed:
"He is here!"

"He is not here,"
Said I, when asked if Christ lived in my heart.
This dear one then to me, the gospel did impart.
Told me how the Son of God left His home in glory –
Was born to a virgin in a manger; a most beautiful story.
Told how He became a man, and dwelt among men,
And was crucified for the remission of my sin.
I invited Him to live in my heart that glorious day.
I'm so thankful that I learned of His righteous way.
And now I can joyfully proclaim:
"He is Here!"

A Rose is Like a Beautiful Face
Charlotte Zotti
The Courtyard
Dayton

A rose is like a beautiful face.
They are most lovely in the spring of the year.
I have had roses in my yard in Atlanta.
I've picked them to give to my neighbors and to
Those who are sick and lonely
To brighten their day.

O, World I Love You So!
Mildred R. Strahley
Asbury Place
Chattanooga

O, world, world, I love you so!

ROCK OF AGES

Your beauty brings me pain –
A pain that poets all must know,
Like sunshine drenched with rain.

O, world, each year you lovelier grow!
How warm God's heart must be!
To give ungrateful people
Such width of shining sea.

So many shining stars at night
To light deep velvet skies,
Shadows, down a moonlit lane,
Bring teardrops to my eyes!

They say that Heaven's lovelier –
Tho' how, I cannot see.
O, world, world I love you so!
Your beauty blesses me!

God's Love
Joyce Huey Salyer
Christian Towers and The Manor of Gallatin
Gallatin

I see God's love in shady green trees
In summertime and honey bees

I see His love in new turned soil
In the work and sweat of the farmer's toil

In water drawn from a country well
It casts on me a magic spell

I see His love in warm sunlight
And even in the still of night

I see His love in works of art
Inspired by a great and holy heart

I see His love in falling rain
Giving life to wheat and grain

I see His love in the ocean wide
Bringing a song with the sound of the tide

I see His love in a little girl
God made this rare and priceless pearl

OUR FAITH

I see His love when Church bells ring
And people gather to pray and sing

I see His love in a Godly mother
Next to Him there is none other

I see Him when the dawn doth break
And from slumber I awake

I thank him for my daily bread
And ask by Him my feet be led

And at the setting of life's sun
I'll thank Him for a race well run.

A Thanksgiving Prayer
Sterling Brownlow
Hewitt House Assisted Living
Pulaski

We are thankful, Lord, for this special day,
And for all good things that come our way.
We are thankful for Jesus Christ, who died for our sins,
And through Him, for us, a new life begins.
We are thankful that He lived on earth and worked,
And his Christian duties, He never shirked.
May we follow the examples that He set
And live by faith, and have no regrets
For the things that we have done or said
And be happy and loving instead.
We are thankful for the Pilgrims, who so long ago,
Set aside a day, their thanks to show.
We know they endured hardships and strife,
In order to have a better way of life.
May we also show our thanks to You
And may our transgressions be very few.
We are indeed thankful for many reasons,
For the approaching Christmas season.
We are here, today, our love for You to reveal
By worshipping You, and having a meal.
We are thankful for the joys we share
We know we have the best country anywhere.
May we always strive good citizens to be,
And always show our love for Thee. Amen.

ROCK OF AGES

I Wonder
Clara Wright
Alexian Brothers Community Services
Chattanooga

The rain, the sunshine and the flowers,
The long, long days and happy hours.
The sleet, the snow and birds soaring high,
Makes me wonder how far is the sky.
But just beyond where man has trod,
The moon, the stars and then there's God.

There's a heaven of splendor in the Bible we're told,
Where the walls are of jasper, the streets are of gold.
And even our loved ones we will meet,
But best of all, our Savior we'll greet.
Each day I give thanks for His wonderful love,
And will praise Him forever in heaven above.

An Ecclesiasticus for Our Day
Phyllis E. Haire
Pine Oaks Assisted Living
Johnson City

I wished to live, live to the hilt;
But I was dead, laid low by guilt.
Then I learned a Savior died for me,
And now I live abundantly.

I wanted might, I wanted power.
Sought them both, each day, each hour.
Then my God made me His own,
Now I go boldly to His throne.

I sought for wealth, all it could bring,
Then of my Lord I learned to sing.
And now through ages yet untold,
I'll walk with Him on streets of gold.

Oh! How I toiled beneath my load,
Then in my heart, He found abode.
And now I walk triumphantly
Because Christ shared His yoke with me.

I tried to ease a troubled heart;
Each passing fad played its part.

OUR FAITH

And then I heard my Savior's call,
And found a peace surpassing all.

Trees

Hildred Hardin
Appalachian Christian Village at Sherwood
Johnson City

Tall and short
Slim and sleek
Fat and chubby
Pretty and ugly
Big and small
Bushy and sprawling
Majestic and graceful –
Sounds like people.

Trees of all sorts,
Descriptions and design.
God made them all
a part of His plan
for a purpose indeed.

Some that give
Some that take
Some that make it
Some that don't.

Long life
Short life
All beautiful in their place
Each unique.

I like the mighty oak
You may like the poplar,
maple, elm, or redbud.

Each to his own.

Shady trees for lazy people
on hot summer days.
Big trees for climbing,
a tree house, or just pure fun.
Tall heavy hardwood trees for building.
Lovely flowering trees
for beauty, aesthetic value.

ROCK OF AGES

Soft and light
for that wood carver
who wants a hobby.
Trees that yield sap
for syrups and oils of
all sorts.
Pulp for the paper,
wood for the fire –
roasting wieners,
and marshmallows, too.

Nuts and fruits and berries
for nourishment's sake.
Evergreen trees
for winter's beauty against the snow,
shelter for animals.
Deep dark wood for those
colorful pieces of furniture.

Each yields and contributes to mankind.
We, too, like the trees,
can offer so much.

We belong.
We are a part of nature.
We do have a place,
a design, a pattern for our needs
and others, too.

Trees all kinds of trees.
People all kinds of people.

Some that yield.
Some that don't.
Some that give.
Some that refuse.
What kind of tree are you?
Stand tall
Fierce and wild
Free and flowing
Bowing and bending with nature.
The elements, that send storms,
sunshine and rain, hail, wind dust
and destruction.
All make the tree.

It is in the bowing and bending
That we manage to survive.
We are made tough.
We are conditioned,

OUR FAITH

Conditioned for the battle of life.

Trees and people.
So much to give.
We, too, like the tree,
must find our place,
Making complete our existence
The harmony of life –
our purpose fulfilled.

Great Tree...
Fill us with your likeness,
Your patience,
Your fulfillment
Your endurance
Your fight and drive
Your strength and might.

Prayer of a Vain Student
  Janella Kirk
  Asbury Place
  Chattanooga

Dear God, please make me
As mighty as can be.
Help me outdo others –
Friends, sisters, brothers.
I want to be head of my class
So let no one else pass.
Make me so very bright
That for honors I need not fight.
I ask again, make me smart
So I won't need to do my part.
Make the teacher a dumb old hen
So I can be her pet. Amen.

Scarlet Ribbon of Pain
  Juanita Vaughan
  Park Place Retirement Community
  Hendersonville

I walk through halls of the wretched,
None know my pain save me;
Not physical pain, but hurt just the same,
Hurt that only the heart may see.

ROCK OF AGES

Pain is a ribbon, a long scarlet ribbon,
The knots are the human life,
Tied, pulled taught with careless hands,
Twisted in the frailness of strife.
Hands reaching, clutching to partake of my strength
Lamenting, "Dear God, why me?"
Entreating, demanding, frightened, commanding,
A miracle setting them free.
In rooms I walk through shadowy valleys,
Hold hands while waters grow still,
Relinquish my hold – into the "Good Shepherd's fold"
Bowing to "Our Father's Will."
A place of dying, a place of great healing,
I rejoice with the many made whole,
Loosing the knots, smoothing rough spots,
A smile on my lips, a tear in my soul.

Easter

Sterling Brownlow
Hewitt House Assisted Living
Pulaski

It seems like but yesterday
That we celebrated Christ's birthday
But, today, we celebrate again
When the Easter season begins
Christ had just His life to give
He gave it that we might live
We celebrate with new Easter bonnets
Or maybe try to write a sonnet
But, may we realize here today
That there is a much better way
We know that time is running out
Maybe we'd better try a different route
As Easter dawns this year
May we feel the presence of the Risen Savior near
And, God, in Thy great wisdom, lead us in a way that's right
And may the darkness of this world be conquered by Thy light.
Before the dawn of Easter, there came Gethsemane
Before the resurrection, there were hours of agony
There can be no crown of stars without a cross to bear
And there is no salvation without faith and love and prayer.
For Jesus suffered, bled and died
That sinners might be sanctified
And to grant God's children such as I
Eternal life in that home on high.

OUR FAITH

My Little Angel
Amber Simmons
Hewitt House Assisted Living
Pulaski

I have a little angel in Heaven I never see.
His little life was taken from him three days before he was born to me.
They said his little face was so disfigured that it was so sad to see.
So my family and the doctor thought it best that I not see.
But his little soul was perfect, perfect as could be.
So he has gone on to Heaven, waiting there for me.
He had a little twin sister, that came on after he.
She was a precious little Darling, and sweet as could be.
Seeing her took away my agony.
She has always been special to all the family,
And always so good, and kind to me.
Now she has grown up and married and is the mother of three.
But she is still so loving and kind, and a blessing to me.

Captain of My Fate
Juanita Vaughan
Park Place Retirement Community
Hendersonville

Lord, guide my feet to pure sweet waters,
Gather me a blue bird there,
One bramble rose, and a day's close,
Forgive all earthly care.
My heart is sick, my soul is bruised,
By wagging tongues of men
Of greedy eyes, of hate, and lies,
Of grasping hands of sin.
While yet I walk the ways of man,
Temptation rules my day,
Fills my dreams with evil schemes,
Lays snares along my way.
Thus I must need go cleanse my soul,
Sit quietly, meditate
"Be still and know that I am God,"
Sweet Captain of my fate.

ROCK OF AGES

Progress?
Sherry S. Haney, R.N.
Adams Place
Murfreesboro

Grandchild of the future
I'm sad to realize
That the things we take for granted
May never feast your eyes.

All the beauty that surrounds us –
Open sky and forest glen
Will have fallen to the dozier
As progress doth descend.

The contractors with big ideas
And the commissioners with their plans
Keep on plotting and dividing
As the money changes hands.

They've forgotten the Great Creator
Seven days He turned His hand
And made this world for creatures, too,
Not exclusively for man.

You may one day hop a rocket
And to Venus go to eat
But it just never will compare
To breakfast at the creek!

Struggle
Edna Buchanan
Sycamores Terrace Retirement Community
Nashville

Without a struggle life would be
A shallow thing for you and me.
Without a struggle there's no goal
To richen and expand the soul;
For with life's hardships we build strength,
And character at greater length.
We need to conquer, not endure,
The knocks that help us to mature;
For if no challenge fired the mind,
Its growth would then lag far behind.
A moth emerging from its case
Would dwarf itself if you'd erase

OUR FAITH

The struggle of its magic birth,
And help it out upon the earth;
For then 'twould prematurely lie,
Quite shriveled, though its wings were dry.
Through human struggle we will find,
Enrichment of both heart and mind;
A meaning thus to life we bring...
For "with no rocks, a brook can't sing."

Flawless?

Joyce Huey Salyer
Christian Towers and The Manor of Gallatin
Gallatin

My Church is not perfect, it has its flaws;
But it stands for God and his dear cause.
The world may say we're no better than they,
But Christians try daily His will to obey.

And I'm only a sinner, but I'm saved by grace
Because on that cross Christ took my place.
The world may think I'm fully insane,
But I've been saved, praise His name!

God's word commands that we love one another;
Oh, precious gems found under that cover.
He has rich, rich blessings for us in store;
He'll fill our lives more and more.
We must empty of self before He'll fill;
He can't use a vessel that's already sealed.
God grant that I may show to the lost
That I've been with Him and counted the cost.

The cost is so little – the reward so great;
Come to Jesus – don't hesitate!
A calm assurance will surely be yours
He has the answers and all the cures.

He won't promise a life without pain,
But he gives sunshine after the rain.
You'll find peace that you never had;
He'll be with you in good times and bad.

Don't you want him – you've a heart to give
Allow the Holy Spirit in you to live.
A pure and sinless Christ lives in me
But I'm still under construction as you can see.

ROCK OF AGES

Now – I Live
Colbert Petrie
Arbor Terrace
Knoxville

When Adam lived, there were flowers
nodding in the breeze;
And trees, young and old, sang their
many-tongued songs.
Streams flowed – some with solemn, somber movement;
Others with joyous, jubilant power, expending their
fresh life recklessly upon anything that opposed them.
Creeping things looked out upon the big world;
And man, the crown of creation, breathed deeply
And felt the earth is good...and God is good!
But I was not there. Not one faint dream
of all that glory came to me,
for my time had not yet come.

When Solomon lived, there were great cities
filled with teeming thousands –
Sad, gay, sincere, deceptive – all kinds
Of people were there, even as today:
And nothing could equal the glory of Solomon
And his court: the beauty of the women,
the splendor of the men!
No, nothing could excel the magnificence
of that court –
Except, perhaps, the lily of the field –
But I was not there. Not one faint dream
of all that glory came to me,
for my time had not yet come.

When Jesus walked the earth, a matchless
Day began to dawn. Shades of evil and ignorance
Drew back, and pallid death lost its horror!
Hope and truth, oft' crushed, dared indeed
to raise their heads and smile again.
Men understood as never before that to live truly,
One must love, and give, and count not the cost –
But I was not there. Not one faint dream
of all that glory came to me,
for my time had not yet come.

But now – today, I live: and I have
tasted life and found it good!
Shall one precious moment pass by meaningless
without flavor or fruit?
Or shall every day be the only day,

OUR FAITH

Full to the brim with worthwhile deeds
and smiles... And love?
Shall every night be the only night –
As though the stars will never shine again,
And the moon but one in a thousand years?
Let me drink the wisdom of the ages,
for my time is here – at last!

Ascent
Faith Cornwall
McKendree Village
Hermitage

Ah, mountains still envelop me,
Filling the nostrils of my mind
With purer breath and memory
Of heights I long had left behind.

Ascending to the hills today
Was more than journeying, I see,
For I am only a higher way;
There is a new expanse in me!

Mother
Amber Simmons
Hewitt House Assisted Living
Pulaski

The word Mother cannot be defined.
You never know what's on her mind.
It's hard to explain,
For it's made up of deep devotion, sacrifice and pain.
Just as Christ shed his blood to give us a new birth,
Mother shed her blood to give us a home on this earth.
Her children are her greatest treasures on this earth,
And it all started on the day of birth.
Sometimes Mother may seem cruel
But other times she's a precious jewel.
A little one can stomp its toe,
And to mother it will always go.
She can love and kiss the pain away,
And it's ready to go back to play.
Mother cannot sleep at night
Until she knows her children are at home and all right.
She just cannot rest for fear

ROCK OF AGES

Something might happen to the ones she loves dear.
Others might forsake you if you go astray,
But Mother never gives up, she will pray and pray.
Although her heart may be breaking,
She just cannot allow her loved one to be forsaken.
Children just cannot understand when they are young and gay,
Just how much mothers worry when they're away.
Sometimes her heart is breaking and she sits alone,
And cries and cries, but with much praying, she always revives.
This is the definition of a mother.
To take her place there is no other.
The reason I know...
I'm a Mother.

Now I Lay Me Down to Sleep
Rose Love Tate
Wesley Highland Manor
Memphis

Prayers have gone out from cathedrals tall
Whose spires reach to the sky
Or prayers perhaps of a broken heart
For some mistake gone by.
Or a mother's prayer for her little brood
As she gathers them in for the night
Asking the Master's guidance
For leading them aright.

Yes, prayers have been said that were only meant
Perhaps for human ears
Or pleas have gone up to the Father
Through penitential tears.

Then there's a prayer that just begins
With simple words, but sweet
It's "Now I lay me down to sleep"
And here let me repeat.

Prayers have gone out from cathedrals tall
That cry the cares of the day
And through their sincere appeal to God
Have surely found their way.

But I believe through Celestial walls
That the ringing noise of the day
Is hushed – and the Father listens and smiles
When a little boy starts to pray.

OUR FAITH

The Hand of God
Ann Anderson
Christian Towers and The Manor of Gallatin
Gallatin

It takes a lifetime to learn how to live,
How to share and how to give.
God takes our hand and leads us through each day,
When sin, sorrow, grief, and tragedy come our way.
How to be brave, and laugh when you want to cry.
We search for answers to the young whose life
Is cut short like a raging sea.
No warning to give their love to their loved ones,
To show them how much they cared.

It takes a lifetime to learn how to live.
How to forgive when your urge is to hate.
But we must forgive today, tomorrow may be too late.
We fall upon our knees and pray,
But sometimes our minds just go astray.
Then God comes and takes our hand,
And leads us through to take our stand;
Giving us hope, security, and peace
With love and happiness to each.

We feel His hand leading the way;
The guiding hand of God is here to stay.

ROCK OF AGES

CHAPTER VII

OUR PAST

One of the most precious gifts our seniors have bestowed on us is their memories. Throughout the history of mankind, the older members of one's family, tribe or society have been valued, even revered, for their memories. It is these memories, imparted to later generations through oral histories or the written word, which give continuity and a sense of tradition to our children and their children. For without these memories, we would soon forget that there ever existed a simpler, more innocent time.

ROCK OF AGES

Memory Lane
Pearl Huntley
Adams Place
Murfreesboro

I love to close my eyes so tight
And walk down memory lane.
There I am just a child again
Playing in the rain.

I see a little girl of three
Wading in the creek.
And peeping 'round a big oak tree,
Playing hide 'n' seek.

I see that little girl at six
Playing April Fool,
And clutching tight her brother's hand
On her first day at school.

I play those memories in my mind.
I know that once again
I can walk backwards down memory lane
Where my heart has always been.

Re-cycled
Sterling Brownlow
Hewitt House Assisted Living
Pulaski

Back in depression times there was little cash,
Now in better times, we're destroying our world with trash
When we were young'uns we re-cycled everything,
Never threw away a single thing.
I remember the containers that came our way,
As vividly as if it were yesterday.
Syrup buckets, the gallon and half-gallon sizes,
We saved them as if they were prizes.
They were good to tote water from the spring,
As lunch boxes to school we'd bring.
We used them if it was cold or hot,
Even used them as a flower pot.
Prince Albert cans held marbles for the boys,
Or maybe buttons, odd lot screws, or other joys.
Cloth sacks held salt, sugar, chicken, and cow feed,
Were used over and over to fill our every need.
We didn't throw away a thing back then,

OUR PAST

Because saving and reusing was a way of life to defend.
It was ingrained in us to waste not, want not,
And to grow something to eat in every little plot.
Bleached out cloth flour and sugar sacks,
Were used as napkins or baby bibs, in fact.
Or petticoats that looked trim and neat,
Especially if it had Yukon's Best across the seat.
Nothing was thrown away, but the chicken bones back then,
And dogs saw to it that they didn't litter again.
We used it up, wore it out,
Made it do, or did without.

Yon End and Back
Pearl Huntley
Adams Place
Murfreesboro

Back in the days when we used those mules
"Yon end and back" was a phrase we used.
When quitting time came, our Dad would say,
"Yon end and back, boys, and we'll call it a day."

Old Bell and Blue knew what he meant, too
Their ears perked up, they knew what to do.
They stepped right out – not a sound was made
They headed for the end and back to the shade.

All of us boys, shirts wet with sweat
Had heard Dad's words we will never forget.
We all had worked hard and done our best
So we are going home now, for food and rest.

Now Dad has passed on, and I miss him a lot
There are so many memories we haven't forgot.
Some are the ones when he'd check around and say,
"Yon end and back, boys, we've made it a day."

ROCK OF AGES

Thanksgiving Stomach Ache
Merle Stanton
Appalachian Christian Village at Sherwood
Johnson City

Thanksgiving I like best
of all the year
'Cause all my kinfolk comes
from far and near.
They bring large platters
of turkey and sauce.
Keep our table full
we have no boss.
No one tells me
to eat this or that.
So I mosey around
and fill myself like a rat.
Last year, though,
wasn't much fun.
I took a pain in my stomach
before I hardly begun.
I ate some turkey,
with a lot of tomatoes.
Then I ate roast beef,
with more potatoes.
Then I had cake,
and cookies galore.
Then I sneaked back
to get some more.
Pumpkin pie
was my delight.
Whipped cream on it
was a beautiful sight.
Oh, mercy me!
I felt a pain.
So I didn't go back
to the table again.
I sneaked back instead,
and lay on the bed.
I rubbed first my belly
and then my head.
Now I'll have to lie here;
can't play or run.
I can't help it,
T'ain't nothing I've done.
But what hurts worst of all,
Dad gummit!
I have to go to bed,
on an empty stomach.

OUR PAST

Learning to Drive
    Mary Miller
    Appalachian Christian Village

    This is something I will never forget. When I was 16 years old, my Mother told me to let my boyfriend teach me how to drive. My Mother had confidence in my boyfriend to teach me because he was an ambulance driver. So on one beautiful Sunday afternoon, my boyfriend and I took my Mother's brand new Studebaker out so I could learn to drive. Of course, my aunt was in the backseat because in those days young ladies took chaperones with them when they saw their boyfriends. Here we went...I get in the car and my boyfriend starts telling me what to do and how to drive. Well, I decided to drive the way I wanted to drive. I was not going to have anyone telling me what to do. So, I tried to drive the car and I flipped it over. Thank goodness no one in the car was seriously hurt. But, the car was totaled and my Mother had only had the car for two weeks! I can remember this happening just like it was yesterday. The moral of the story is "Always mind your Mother."

Courting in Cardboard Soles
    Pearl Huntley
    Adams Place
    Murfreesboro

Back in the thirties when love was young
Wasn't much money, but still we had fun.
Not many clothes, our shoes full of holes,
We went a'courting in cardboard soles.

Yes, there was many a bread line, see.
But folks got along fine, that is, mostly.
For we had plenty of corn bread and jowls
And we went a'courting in cardboard soles.

"Prosperity's around the corner," we heard,
But a body can't make a living by word.
So folks went a'fishing with their poles
And we went a'courting in cardboard soles.

Jobs were hard to find back in them days.
Still, folks laughed and cried and loved always.
Then, as always, they had dreams and goals.
And we went a'courting in cardboard soles.

ROCK OF AGES

A Christmas Gift
Rose Love Tate
Wesley Highland Manor
Memphis

Some time ago I spent hours,
As busy as I could be
Trying to find something special
To put on your Christmas tree.

Times have changed and I must decide
What am I going to do
It may be a little different
That is all so true.
But it's something that I give freely,
Especially just for you.

It won't be wrapped in tissues,
Nor tied with a fancy bow
There's no box large enough to hold it
That's all so true, you know.

But it's something from my heart
All sincere and true
My very special Christmas love
Especially for you!

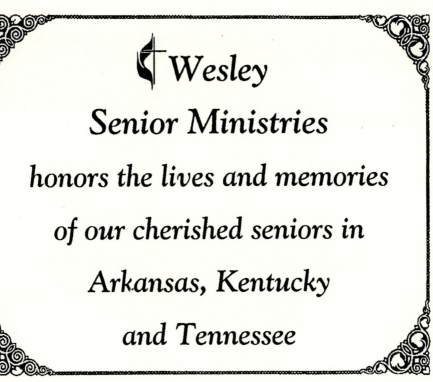

Tennessee Association of Homes and Services for the Aging
500 Interstate Blvd. South, Nashville, TN 37201
615-256-1800 (phone)
615-726-3082 (fax)
dpace@tha.com (email)

A tremendous debt of
gratitude goes out to all Tennessee's older
adults who shared their experiences, imparted
their wisdom and expressed their lives to
make *Rock of Ages* and to make sure we
never forget.

ALEXIAN BROTHERS
COMMUNITY SERVICES
Program of All-inclusive Care for the Elderly PACE

HOME
Medical
1-800-489-1911

Providing patient care, equipment and supplies to Western & Middle Tennessee

The Air Conditioning Specialists
LISSCO

Lawrence Independent Sales & Service Co.
P.O. Box 10568   Knoxville, TN 37939
1-800-4-LISSCO   (800-454-7726)
local: (865) 633-5109   fax: (865) 633-5265

Specialists in Self Contained Air Conditioning Products, Ventilation Products, Package Terminal Air Conditioners and Heat Pumps

Call
1-800-454-7726

Sales • Service • Parts

Visit our Website at www.LISSCOac.com

Ambulance Services, Inc.
1-800-489-1033

Memphis, Nashville, Franklin, Waverly, Perry

❄Appalachian Christian Village

Your hometown, not-for-profit, retirement and senior living organization...

Sherwood

...a retirement community for a more independent and active lifestyle with choice of townhouses, luxury apartments, and congregate apartments

Pine Oaks

...an assisted living community promoting wellness and independence with 24 hour licensed practical nurses

Health Care Center

...a Level I (intermediate) licensed nursing facility providing long-term, short-term, and respite care services

In Home Services

...providing an option to encourage and promote independence with services that come directly to your home, retirement center, nursing home, or hospital...

423-610-8508

www.christianvillage.org

Call today for more information regarding Appalachian Christian Village's services to seniors and their families.

Our mission is to reflect Christ's love.